Atlanta Braves 2021

A Baseball Companion

Edited by Steven Goldman and Bret Sayre

Baseball Prospectus

Craig Brown, Associate Editor
Robert Au, Harry Pavlidis and Amy Pircher, Statistics Editors

Copyright © 2021 by DIY Baseball, LLC.
All rights reserved

This book or any part thereof may not be reproduced or transmitted in any form or by any means, electronic or mechanical, including photocopying, recording, or by any information storage and retrieval system, without permission in writing from the publisher.

Limit of Liability/Disclaimer of Warranty: While the publisher and the author have used their best efforts in preparing this book, they make no representations or warranties with respect to the accuracy or completeness of the contents of this book and specifically disclaim any implied warranties of merchantability or fitness for a particular purpose. No warranty may be created or extended by sales representatives or written sales materials. The advice and strategies contained herein may not be suitable for your situation. You should consult with a professional where appropriate. Neither the publisher nor the author shall be liable for any loss of profit or any other commercial damages, including but not limited to special, incidental, consequential, or other damages.

Library of Congress Cataloging-in-Publication Data:
paperback
ISBN-13: 978-1-950716-27-2

Project Credits
Cover Design: Ginny Searle
Interior Design and Production: Amy Pircher, Robert Au
Layout: Amy Pircher, Robert Au

Baseball icon courtesy of Uberux, from https://www.shareicon.net/author/uberux

Ballpark diagram courtesy of Lou Spirito/THIRTY81 Project, https://thirty81project.com/

Manufactured in the United States of America
10 9 8 7 6 5 4 3 2 1

Table of Contents

Statistical Introduction v

Part 1: Team Analysis

Performance Graphs 3

2020 Team Performance 4

2021 Team Projections 5

Team Personnel 6

SunTrust Park Stats 7

Braves Team Analysis 9

Part 2: Player Analysis

Braves Player Analysis 16

Braves Prospects 105

Part 3: Featured Articles

Braves All-Time Top 10 Players 119
    by Matthew Trueblood

A Taxonomy of 2020 Abnormalities 125
    by Rob Mains

Tranches of WAR 131
    by Russell A. Carleton

Secondhand Sport 137
    by Patrick Dubuque

Steve Dalkowski Dreaming 141
    by Steven Goldman

A Reward For A Functioning Society 145
    by Cory Frontin and Craig Goldstein

Index of Names 149

Statistical Introduction

Sports are, fundamentally, a blend of athletic endeavor and storytelling. Baseball, like any other sport, tells its stories in so many ways: in the arc of a game from the stands or a season from the box scores, in photos, or even in numbers. At Baseball Prospectus, we understand that statistics don't replace observation or any of baseball's stories, but complement everything else that makes the game so much fun.

What stats help us with is with patterns and precision, variance and value. This book can help you learn things you may not see from watching a game or hundred, whether it's the path of a career over time or the breadth of the entire MLB. We'd also never ask you to choose between our numbers and the experience of viewing a game from the cheap seats or the comfort of your home; our publication combines running the numbers with observations and wisdom from some of the brightest minds we can find. But if you *do* want to learn more about the numbers beyond what's on the backs of player jerseys, let us help explain.

Offense

We've revised our methodology for determining batting value. Long-time readers of the book will notice that we've retired True Average in favor of a new metric: Deserved Runs Created Plus (DRC+). Developed by Jonathan Judge and our stats team, this statistic measures everything a player does at the plate–reaching base, hitting for power, making outs, and moving runners over–and puts it on a scale where 100 equals league-average performance. A DRC+ of 150 is terrific, a DRC+ of 100 is average and a DRC+ of 75 means you better be an excellent defender.

DRC+ also does a better job than any of our previous metrics in taking contextual factors into account. The model adjusts for how the park affects performance, but also for things like the talent of the opposing pitcher, value of different types of batted-ball events, league, temperature and other factors. It's able to describe a player's expected offensive contribution than any other statistic we've found over the years, and also does a better job of predicting future performance as well.

The other aspect of run-scoring is baserunning, which we quantify using Baserunning Runs. BRR not only records the value of stolen bases (or getting caught in the act), but also accounts for all the stuff that doesn't show up on the back of a baseball card: a runner's ability to go first to third on a single, or advance on a fly ball.

Defense

Where offensive value is *relatively* easy to identify and understand, defensive value is ... not. Over the past dozen years, the sabermetric community has focused mostly on stats based on zone data: a real-live human person records the type of batted ball and estimated landing location, and models are created that give expected outs. From there, you can compare fielders' actual outs to those expected ones. Simple, right?

Unfortunately, zone data has two major issues. First, zone data is recorded by commercial data providers who keep the raw data private unless you pay for it. (All the statistics we build in this book and on our website use public data as inputs.) That hurts our ability to test assumptions or duplicate results. Second, over the years it has become apparent that there's quite a bit of "noise" in zone-based fielding analysis. Sometimes the conclusions drawn from zone data don't hold up to scrutiny, and sometimes the different data provided by different providers don't look anything alike, giving wildly different results. Sometimes the hard-working professional stringers or scorers might unknowingly inflict unconscious bias into the mix: for example good fielders will often be credited with more expected outs despite the data, and ballparks with high press boxes tend to score more line drives than ones with a lower press box.

Enter our Fielding Runs Above Average (FRAA). For most positions, FRAA is built from play-by-play data, which allows us to avoid the subjectivity found in many other fielding metrics. The idea is this: count how many fielding plays are made by a given player and compare that to expected plays for an average fielder at their position (based on pitcher ground ball tendencies and batter handedness). Then we adjust for park and base-out situations.

When it comes to catchers, our methodology is a little different thanks to the laundry list of responsibilities they're tasked with beyond just, well, catching and throwing the ball. By now you've probably heard about "framing" or the art of making umpires more likely to call balls outside the strike zone for strikes. To put this into one tidy number, we incorporate pitch tracking data (for the years it exists) and adjust for important factors like pitcher, umpire, batter and home-field advantage using a mixed-model approach. This grants us a number for how many strikes the catcher is personally adding to (or subtracting from) his pitchers' performance ... which we then convert to runs added or lost using linear weights.

Framing is one of the biggest parts of determining catcher value, but we also take into account blocking balls from going past, whether a scorer deems it a passed ball or a wild pitch. We use a similar approach—one that really benefits from the pitch tracking data that tells us what ends up in the dirt and what doesn't. We also include a catcher's ability to prevent stolen bases and how well they field balls in play, and *finally* we come up with our FRAA for catchers.

Pitching

Both pitching and fielding make up the half of baseball that isn't run scoring: run prevention. Separating pitching from fielding is a tough task, and most recent pitching analysis has branched off from Voros McCracken's famous (and controversial) statement, "There is little if any difference among major-league pitchers in their ability to prevent hits on balls hit in the field of play." The research of the analytic community has validated this to some extent, and there are a host of "defense-independent" pitching measures that have been developed to try and extract the effect of the defense behind a hurler from the pitcher's work.

Our solution to this quandary is Deserved Run Average (DRA), our core pitching metric. DRA seeks to evaluate a pitcher's performance, much like earned run average (ERA), the tried-and-true pitching stat you've seen on every baseball broadcast or box score from the past century, but it's very different. To start, DRA takes an event-by-event look at what the pitchers does, and adjusts the value of that event based on different environmental factors like park, batter, catcher, umpire, base-out situation, run differential, inning, defense, home field advantage, pitcher role and temperature. That mixed model gives us a pitcher's expected contribution, similar to what we do for our DRC+ model for hitters and FRAA model for catchers. (Oh, and we also consider the pitcher's effect on basestealing and on balls getting past the catcher.)

DRA is set to the scale of runs allowed per nine innings (RA9) instead of ERA, which makes DRA's scale slightly higher than ERA's. Because of this, for ease of use, we're supplying DRA-, which is much easier for the reader to parse. As with DRC+, DRA- is an "index" stat, meaning instead of using some arbitrary and shifting number to denote what's "good," average is always 100. The reason that it uses a minus rather than a plus is because like ERA, a lower number is better. Therefore a 75 DRA- describes a performance 25 percent better than average, whereas a 150 DRA- means that either a pitcher is getting extremely lucky with their results, or getting ready to try a new pitch.

Since the last time you picked up an edition of this book, we've also made a few minor changes to DRA to make it better. Recent research into "tunneling"—the act of throwing consecutive pitches that appear similar from a batter's point of view until after the swing decision point–data has given us a new contextual factor to account for in DRA: plate distance. This refers to the distance between successive pitches as they approach the plate, and while it has a smaller effect than factors like velocity or whiff rate, it still can help explain pitcher strikeout rate in our model.

Recently Added Descriptive Statistics

Returning to our 2021 edition of the book are a few figures which recently appeared. These numbers may be a little bit more familiar to those of you who have spent some time investigating baseball statistics.

Fastball Percentage

Our fastball percentage (FA%) statistic measures how frequently a pitcher throws a pitch classified as a "fastball," measured as a percentage of overall pitches thrown. We qualify three types of fastballs:

1. The traditional four-seam fastball;
2. The two-seam fastball or sinker;
3. "Hard cutters," which are pitches that have the movement profile of a cut fastball and are used as the pitcher's primary offering or in place of a more traditional fastball.

For example, a pitcher with a FA% of 67 throws any combination of these three pitches about two-thirds of the time.

Whiff Rate

Everybody loves a swing and a miss, and whiff rate (Whiff%) measures how frequently pitchers induce a swinging strike. To calculate Whiff%, we add up all the pitches thrown that ended with a swinging strike, then divide that number by a pitcher's total pitches thrown. Most often, high whiff rates correlate with high strikeout rates (and overall effective pitcher performance).

Called Strike Probability

Called Strike Probability (CSP) is a number that represents the likelihood that all of a pitcher's pitches will be called a strike while controlling for location, pitcher and batter handedness, umpire and count. Here's how it works: on each pitch, our model determines how many times (out of 100) that a similar pitch was called for a strike given those factors mentioned above, and when normalized for each batter's strike zone. Then we average the CSP for all pitches thrown by a pitcher in a season, and that gives us the yearly CSP percentage you see in the stats boxes.

As you might imagine, pitchers with a higher CSP are more likely to work in the zone, where pitchers with a lower CSP are likely locating their pitches outside the normal strike zone, for better or for worse.

Projections

Many of you aren't turning to this book just for a look at what a player has done, but for a look at what a player is going to do: the PECOTA projections. PECOTA, initially developed by Nate Silver (who has moved on to greater fame as a political analyst), consists of three parts:

1. Major-league equivalencies, which use minor-league statistics to project how a player will perform in the major leagues;
2. Baseline forecasts, which use weighted averages and regression to the mean to estimate a player's current true talent level; and
3. Aging curves, which uses the career paths of comparable players to estimate how a player's statistics are likely to change over time.

With all those important things covered, let's take a look at what's in the book this year.

Team Prospectus

Most of this book is composed of team chapters, with one for each of the 30 major-league franchises. On the first page of each chapter, you'll see a box that contains some of the key statistics for each team as well as a very inviting stadium diagram.

We start with the team name, their unadjusted 2020 win-loss record, and their divisional ranking. Beneath that are a host of other team statistics. **Pythag** presents an adjusted 2020 winning percentage, calculated by taking runs scored per game (**RS/G**) and runs allowed per game (**RA/G**) for the team, and running them through a version of Bill James' Pythagorean formula that was refined and improved by David Smyth and Brandon Heipp. (The formula is called "Pythagenpat," which is equally fun to type and to say.)

Next up is **DRC+**, described earlier, to indicate the overall hitting ability of the team either above or below league-average. Run prevention on the pitching side is covered by **DRA** (also mentioned earlier) and another metric: Fielding Independent Pitching (**FIP**), which calculates another ERA-like statistic based on strikeouts, walks, and home runs recorded. Defensive Efficiency Rating (**DER**) tells us the percentage of balls in play turned into outs for the team, and is a quick fielding shorthand that rounds out run prevention.

After that, we have several measures related to roster composition, as opposed to on-field performance. **B-Age** and **P-Age** tell us the average age of a team's batters and pitchers, respectively. **Payroll** is the combined team payroll for all on-field players, and Doug Pappas' Marginal Dollars per Marginal Win (**M$/MW**) tells us how much money a team spent to earn production above replacement level.

Next to each of these stats, we've listed each team's MLB rank in that category from first to 30th. In this, first always indicates a positive outcome and 30th a negative outcome, except in the case of salary—first is highest.

After the franchise statistics, we share a few items about the team's home ballpark. There's the aforementioned diagram of the park's dimensions (including distances to the outfield wall), a graphic showing the height of the wall from the left-field pole to the right-field pole, and a table showing three-year park factors for the stadium. The park factors are displayed as indexes where 100 is average, 110 means that the park inflates the statistic in question by 10 percent, and 90 means that the park deflates the statistic in question by 10 percent.

On the second page of each team chapter, you'll find three graphs. The first is **Payroll History** and helps you see how the team's payroll has compared to the MLB and divisional average payrolls over time. Payroll figures are current as of January 1, 2021; with so many free agents still unsigned as of this writing, the final 2021 figure will likely be significantly different for many teams. (In the meantime, you can always find the most current data at Baseball Prospectus' Cot's Baseball Contracts page.)

The second graph is **Future Commitments** and helps you see the team's future outlays, if any.

The third graph is **Farm System Ranking** and displays how the Baseball Prospectus prospect team has ranked the organization's farm system since 2007.

After the graphs, we have a **Personnel** section that lists many of the important decision-makers and upper-level field and operations staff members for the franchise, as well as any former Baseball Prospectus staff members who are currently part of the organization. (In very rare circumstances, someone might be on both lists!)

Position Players

After all that information and a thoughtful bylined essay covering each team, we present our player comments. These are also bylined, but due to frequent franchise shifts during the offseason, our bylines are more a rough guide than a perfect accounting of who wrote what.

Each player is listed with the major-league team that employed him as of early January 2021. If a player changed teams after that point via free agency, trade, or any other method, you'll be able to find them in the chapter for their previous squad.

As an example, take a look at the player comment for Padres shortstop Fernando Tatis Jr.: the stat block that accompanies his written comment is at the top of this page. First we cover biographical information (age is as of June 30, 2021) before moving onto the stats themselves. Our statistic columns include standard identifying information like **YEAR**, **TEAM**, **LVL** (level of affiliated play) and **AGE** before getting into the numbers. Next, we provide raw, untranslated

Fernando Tatis Jr. SS

Born: 01/02/99   Age: 22   Bats: R   Throws: R
Height: 6'3"   Weight: 217   Origin: International Free Agent, 2015

YEAR	TEAM	LVL	AGE	PA	R	2B	3B	HR	RBI	BB	K	SB	CS	AVG/OBP/SLG
2018	SA	AA	19	394	77	22	4	16	43	33	109	16	5	.286/.355/.507
2019	SD	MLB	20	372	61	13	6	22	53	30	110	16	6	.317/.379/.590
2020	SD	MLB	21	257	50	11	2	17	45	27	61	11	3	.277/.366/.571
2021 FS	SD	MLB	22	600	95	24	4	31	81	50	165	17	8	.263/.331/.499
2021 DC	SD	MLB	22	628	100	25	4	32	85	53	173	19	8	.263/.331/.499

Comparables: Darryl Strawberry, Bo Bichette, Ronald Acuña Jr.

YEAR	TEAM	LVL	AGE	PA	DRC+	BABIP	BRR	FRAA	WARP
2018	SA	AA	19	394	136	.370	3.0	SS(83): -1.9	2.4
2019	SD	MLB	20	372	118	.410	7.1	SS(83): 0.9	3.4
2020	SD	MLB	21	257	126	.306	0.7	SS(57): -5.5	0.9
2021 FS	SD	MLB	22	600	126	.318	1.7	SS -1	3.9
2021 DC	SD	MLB	22	628	126	.318	1.8	SS -1	4.0

numbers like you might find on the back of your dad's baseball cards: **PA** (plate appearances), **R** (runs), **2B** (doubles), **3B** (triples), **HR** (home runs), **RBI** (runs batted in), **BB** (walks), **K** (strikeouts), **SB** (stolen bases) and **CS** (caught stealing).

Following the basic stats is **Whiff%** (whiff rate), which denotes how often, when a batter swings, he fails to make contact with the ball. Another way to think of this number is an inverse of a hitter's contact rate.

Next, we have unadjusted "slash" statistics: **AVG** (batting average), **OBP** (on-base percentage) and **SLG** (slugging percentage). Following the slash line is **DRC+** (Deserved Runs Created Plus), which we described earlier as total offensive expected contribution compared to the league average.

BABIP (batting average on balls in play) tells us how often a ball in play fell for a hit, and can help us identify whether a batter may have been lucky or not ... but note that high BABIPs also tend to follow the great hitters of our time, as well as speedy singles hitters who put the ball on the ground.

The next item is **BRR** (Baserunning Runs), which covers all of a player's baserunning accomplishments including (but not limited to) swiped bags and failed attempts. Next is **FRAA** (Fielding Runs Above Average), which also includes the number of games previously played at each position noted in parentheses. Multi-position players have only their two most frequent positions listed here, but their total FRAA number reflects all positions played.

Our last column here is **WARP** (Wins Above Replacement Player). WARP estimates the total value of a player, which means for hitters it takes into account hitting runs above average (calculated using the DRC+ model), BRR and FRAA. Then, it makes an adjustment for positions played and gives the player a credit

Atlanta Braves 2021

for plate appearances based upon the difference between "replacement level"—which is derived from the quality of players added to a team's roster after the start of the season–and the league average.

The final line just below the stats box is **PECOTA** data, which is discussed further in a following section.

Catchers

Catchers are a special breed, and thus they have earned their own separate box which displays some of the defensive metrics that we've built just for them. As an example, let's check out Yasmani Grandal.

YEAR	TEAM	P. COUNT	FRM RUNS	BLK RUNS	THRW RUNS	TOT RUNS
2018	LAD	16816	15.7	0.8	0.1	16.5
2019	MIL	18740	19.4	1.8	-0.1	21.1
2020	CHW	4830	3.7	0.3	-0.2	3.8
2021	CHW	14430	16.7	-0.6	1.0	17.1
2021	CHW	14430	16.7	0.4	1.0	18.0

The **YEAR** and **TEAM** columns match what you'd find in the other stat box. **P. COUNT** indicates the number of pitches thrown while the catcher was behind the plate, including swinging strikes, fouls and balls in play. **FRM RUNS** is the total run value the catcher provided (or cost) his team by influencing the umpire to call strikes where other catchers did not. **BLK RUNS** expresses the total run value above or below average for the catcher's ability to prevent wild pitches and passed balls. **THRW RUNS** is calculated using a similar model as the previous two statistics, and it measures a catcher's ability to throw out basestealers but also to dissuade them from testing his arm in the first place. It takes into account factors like the pitcher (including his delivery and pickoff move) and baserunner (who could be as fast as Billy Hamilton or as slow as Yonder Alonso). **TOT RUNS** is the sum of all of the previous three statistics.

Pitchers

Let's give our pitchers a turn, using 2020 AL Cy Young winner Shane Bieber as our example. Take a look at his stat block: the first line and the **YEAR**, **TEAM**, **LVL** and **AGE** columns are the same as in the position player example earlier.

Here too, we have a series of columns that display raw, unadjusted statistics compiled by the pitcher over the course of a season: **W** (wins), **L** (losses), **SV** (saves), **G** (games pitched), **GS** (games started), **IP** (innings pitched), **H** (hits allowed) and **HR** (home runs allowed). Next we have two statistics that are rates: **BB/9** (walks per nine innings) and **K/9** (strikeouts per nine innings), before returning to the unadjusted K (strikeouts).

Next up is **GB%** (ground ball percentage), which is the percentage of all batted balls that were hit on the ground, including both outs and hits. Remember, this is based on observational data and subject to human error, so please approach this with a healthy dose of skepticism.

BABIP (batting average on balls in play) is calculated using the same methodology as it is for position players, but it often tells us more about a pitcher than it does a hitter. With pitchers, a high BABIP is often due to poor defense or bad luck, and can often be an indicator of potential rebound, and a low BABIP may be cause to expect performance regression. (A typical league-average BABIP is close to .290-.300.)

The metrics **WHIP** (walks plus hits per inning pitched) and **ERA** (earned run average) are old standbys: WHIP measures walks and hits allowed on a per-inning basis, while ERA measures earned runs on a nine-inning basis. Neither of these stats are translated or adjusted.

DRA- (Deserved Run Average) was described at length earlier, and measures how the pitcher "deserved" to perform compared to other pitchers. Please note that since we lack all the data points that would make for a "real" DRA for minor-league events, the DRA- displayed for minor league partial-seasons is based off of different data. (That data is a modified version of our cFIP metric, which you can find more information about on our website.)

Shane Bieber   RHP

Born: 05/31/95   Age: 26   Bats: R   Throws: R
Height: 6'3"   Weight: 200   Origin: Round 4, 2016 Draft (#122 overall)

YEAR	TEAM	LVL	AGE	W	L	SV	G	GS	IP	H	HR	BB/9	K/9	K	GB%	BABIP
2018	AKR	AA	23	3	0	0	5	5	31	26	1	0.3	8.7	30	47.3%	.278
2018	COL	AAA	23	3	1	0	8	8	48²	30	3	1.1	8.7	47	52.0%	.227
2018	CLE	MLB	23	11	5	0	20	19	114²	130	13	1.8	9.3	118	46.2%	.356
2019	CLE	MLB	24	15	8	0	34	33	214¹	186	31	1.7	10.9	259	44.4%	.298
2020	CLE	MLB	25	8	1	0	12	12	77¹	46	7	2.4	14.2	122	48.4%	.267
2021 FS	CLE	MLB	26	10	6	0	26	26	150	121	18	2.1	11.7	195	45.5%	.297
2021 DC	CLE	MLB	26	14	7	0	30	30	196.7	159	24	2.1	11.7	257	45.5%	.297

Comparables: Luis Severino, Danny Salazar, Joe Musgrove

YEAR	TEAM	LVL	AGE	WHIP	ERA	DRA-	WARP	MPH	FB%	WHF	CSP
2018	AKR	AA	23	0.87	1.16	61	0.9				
2018	COL	AAA	23	0.74	1.66	69	1.2				
2018	CLE	MLB	23	1.33	4.55	74	2.6	94.7	57.4%	26.2%	
2019	CLE	MLB	24	1.05	3.28	75	4.9	94.4	45.8%	30.8%	
2020	CLE	MLB	25	0.87	1.63	53	2.6	95.3	53.6%	40.7%	
2021 FS	CLE	MLB	26	1.04	2.44	64	4.4	94.7	50.0%	33.2%	44.2%
2021 DC	CLE	MLB	26	1.04	2.44	64	5.8	94.7	50.0%	33.2%	44.2%

Just like with hitters, **WARP** (Wins Above Replacement Player) is a total value metric that puts pitchers of all stripes on the same scale as position players. We use DRA as the primary input for our calculation of WARP. You might notice that relief pitchers (due to their limited innings) may have a lower WARP than you were expecting or than you might see in other WARP-like metrics. WARP does not take leverage into account, just the actions a pitcher performs and the expected value of those actions ... which ends up judging high-leverage relief pitchers differently than you might imagine given their prestige and market value.

MPH gives you the pitcher's 95th percentile velocity for the noted season, in order to give you an idea of what the *peak* fastball velocity a pitcher possesses. Since this comes from our pitch-tracking data, it is not publicly available for minor-league pitchers.

Finally, we display the three new pitching metrics we described earlier. **FB%** (fastball percentage) gives you the percentage of fastballs thrown out of all pitches. **WHF** (whiff rate) tells you the percentage of swinging strikes induced out of all pitches. **CSP** (called strike probability) expresses the likelihood of all pitches thrown to result in a called strike, after controlling for factors like handedness, umpire, pitch type, count and location.

PECOTA

All players have PECOTA projections for 2021, as well as a set of other numbers that describe the performance of comparable players according to PECOTA. All projections for 2021 are for the player at the date we went to press in early January and are projected into the league and park context as indicated by the team abbreviation. (Note that players at very low levels of the minors are too unpredictable to assess using these numbers.) All PECOTA projected statistics represent a player's projected major-league performance.

How we're doing that is a little different this season. There are really two different values that go into the final stat line that you see for PECOTA: How a player performs, and how much playing time he'll be given to perform it. In the past we've estimated playing time based on each team's roster and depth charts, and we'll continue to do that. These projections are denoted as **2021 DC**.

But in many cases, a player won't be projected for major-league playing time; most of the time this is because they aren't projected to be major-league players at all, but still developing as prospects. Or perhaps a player will provide Triple-A depth, only to have an opportunity open up because of injury. For these purposes, we're also supplying a second projection, labeled **2021 FS**, or full season. This is what we would project the player to provide in 600 plate appearances or 150 innings pitched.

Below the projections are the player's three highest-scoring comparable players as determined by PECOTA. All comparables represent a snapshot of how the listed player was performing at the same age as the current player, so if a

23-year-old pitcher is compared to Bartolo Colón, he's actually being compared to a 23-year-old Colón, not the version that pitched for the Rangers in 2018, nor to Colón's career as a whole.

A few points about pitcher projections. First, we aren't yet projecting peak velocity, so that column will be blank in the PECOTA lines. Second, projecting DRA is trickier than evaluating past performance, because it is unclear how deserving each pitcher will be of his anticipated outcomes. However, we know that another DRA-related statistic–contextual FIP or cFIP-estimates future run scoring very well. So for PECOTA, the projected DRA- figures you see are based on the past cFIPs generated by the pitcher and comparable players over time, along with the other factors described above.

If you're familiar with PECOTA, then you'll have noticed that the projection system often appears bullish on players coming off a bad year and bearish on players coming off a good year. (This is because the system weights several previous seasons, not just the most recent one.) In addition, we publish the 50th percentile projections for each player–which is smack in the middle of the range of projected production—which tends to mean PECOTA stat lines don't often have extreme results like 40 home runs or 250 strikeouts in a given season. In essence, PECOTA doesn't project very many extreme seasons.

Managers

After all those wonderful team chapters, we've got statistics for each big-league manager, all of whom are organized by alphabetical order. Here you'll find a block including an extraordinary amount of information collected from each manager's entire career. For more information on the acronyms and what they mean, please visit the Glossary at www.baseballprospectus.com.

There is one important metric that we'd like to call attention to, and you'll find it next to each manager's name: **wRM+** (weighted reliever management plus). Developed by Rob Arthur and Rian Watt, wRM+ investigates how good a manager is at using their best relievers during the moments of highest leverage, using both our proprietary DRA metric as well as Leverage Index. wRM+ is scaled to a league average of 100, and a wRM+ of 105 indicates that relievers were used approximately five percent "better" than average. On the other hand, a wRM+ of 95 would tell us the team used its relievers five percent "worse" than the average team.

While wRM+ does not have an extremely strong correlation with a manager, it is statistically significant; this means that a manager is not *entirely* responsible for a team's wRM+, but does have some effect on that number.

Part 1: Team Analysis

Performance Graphs

Payroll History (in millions)

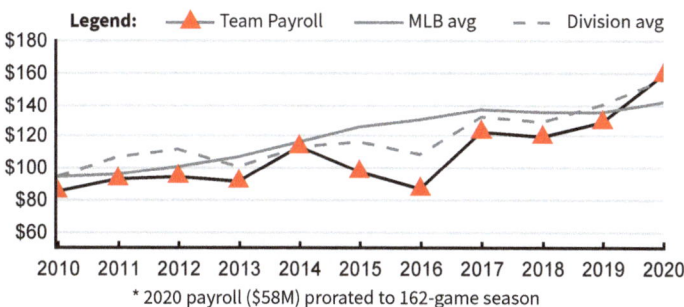

Future Commitments (in millions)

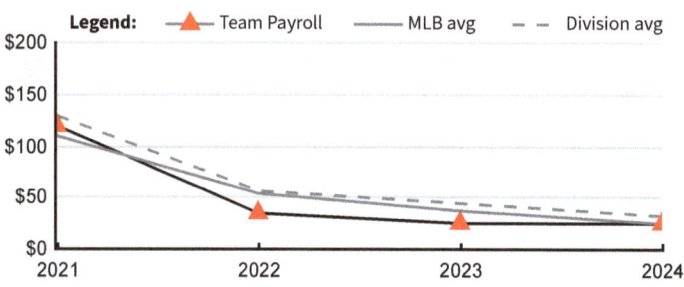

Farm System Ranking

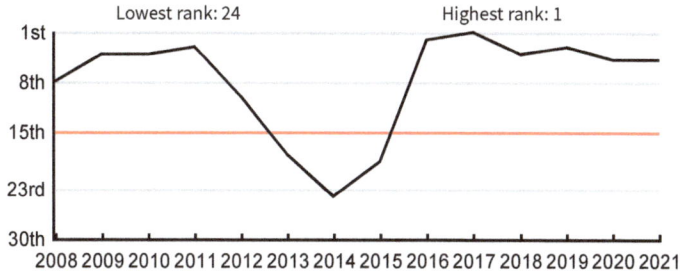

2020 Team Performance

ACTUAL STANDINGS

Team	W	L	Pct
ATL	**35**	**25**	**0.583**
MIA	31	29	0.517
PHI	28	32	0.467
NYM	26	34	0.433
WAS	26	34	0.433

dWIN% STANDINGS

Team	W	L	Pct
PHI	34	26	0.580
ATL	**33**	**27**	**0.562**
NYM	32	28	0.549
WAS	27	33	0.450
MIA	25	35	0.431

TOP HITTERS

Player	WARP
Freddie Freeman	2.6
Marcell Ozuna	2.4
Ronald Acuña Jr.	1.8

TOP PITCHERS

Player	WARP
Max Fried	1.1
Tyler Matzek	0.9
Ian Anderson	0.9

VITAL STATISTICS

Statistic Name	Value	Rank
Pythagenpat	.592	6th
dWin%	.562	4th
Runs Scored per Game	5.80	2nd
Runs Allowed per Game	4.80	15th
Deserved Runs Created Plus	115	2nd
Deserved Run Average Minus	98	14th
Fielding Independent Pitching	4.42	13th
Defensive Efficiency Rating	.693	21st
Batter Age	28.7	11th
Pitcher Age	28.9	12th
Payroll	$58.0M	14th
Marginal $ per Marginal Win	$2.4M	10th

2021 Team Projections

PROJECTED STANDINGS

Team	W	L	Pct	+/-
NYM	93.6	68.4	0.578	23
Their additions should yield the best Mets team since 2015, even if their competition in the NL East is much stiffer than it was then.				
WAS	84.7	77.3	0.523	14
Mike Rizzo remade the middle of his lineup and improved the pitching staff, but given the caliber of their competition he could have aimed a hair higher.				
PHI	83.8	78.2	0.517	8
Re-signing J.T. Realmuto and Didi Gregorius keeps the offense intact, but has Dave Dombrowski successfully built a bullpen?				
ATL	81.5	80.5	0.503	-13
The rotation and positional stars set a high floor; their role players will determine their ceiling.				
MIA	70.9	91.1	0.438	-12
Hired a transformational leader and then did nothing to improve (or even reshape) a middling roster.				

TOP PROJECTED HITTERS

Player	WARP
Freddie Freeman	5.3
Ronald Acuña Jr.	5.1
Marcell Ozuna	3.7

TOP PROJECTED PITCHERS

Player	WARP
Charlie Morton	2.2
Max Fried	2.0
Mike Soroka	2.0

FARM SYSTEM REPORT

Top Prospect	Number of Top 101 Prospects
Ian Anderson, #5	5

KEY DEDUCTIONS

Player	WARP
Darren O'Day	0.8

KEY ADDITIONS

Player	WARP
Charlie Morton	2.2
Drew Smyly	1.1
Victor Arano	0.3

Team Personnel

Executive Vice President, General Manager
Alex Anthopoulos

Assistant General Manager, Research and Development
Jason Paré

Assistant General Manager, Player Development
Ben Sestanovich

Special Assistant to the General Manager
Mike Fast

Manager
Brian Snitker

BP Alumni
Mike Fast
Jason Paré
Ronit Shah
Noah Woodward
Colin Wyers

SunTrust Park Stats

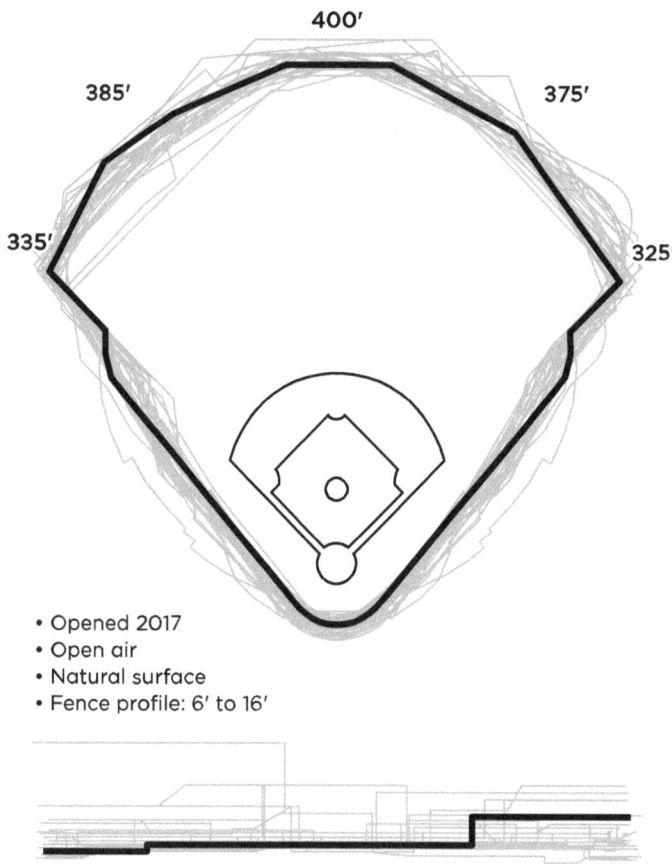

- Opened 2017
- Open air
- Natural surface
- Fence profile: 6' to 16'

Three-Year Park Factors

Runs	Runs/RH	Runs/LH	HR/RH	HR/LH
102	101	105	94	100

Braves Team Analysis

By the third inning of the fifth game of the National League Championship Series, it felt as inevitable as a playoff game can feel. Atlanta was up 3-1 in the series, and they looked good. The bats were hot, the fielding was quick, the energy in the dugout was dry kindling just waiting for a match to explode in a roar that would take down the Dodgers once again, and propel Atlanta into the World Series. The inning started with promise. The Braves were up by two runs already and bing, bang, boom the first two runners hit singles. A ground out moved them to second and third. Isn't that beautiful? When good baseball is played, and a professional sacrifices being the hero to move his buddies into scoring position. It felt good.

I sat up from my reclined position on my couch, moved the scorebook I'd been using all season to try and focus on the games to the coffee table, and leaned forward, elbows on my knees. It just needed a match. One measly match. You could feel it in the air, even through the television. You could see it in the quick bounce of Dansby Swanson's batting stance. Did he feel it too? He must, because here came the first pitch out of Joe Kelly's hand, swirling down toward the plate, and he had the green light. Swanson swung and his bat arced through the zone, no radiation on his hands, all firm contact on that breaking pitch, so that it ricocheted away from the batter's box and far over Kelly's head. A Texas Leaguer! It was falling so quickly, popping right into that no man's land that no shift can fully cover between the infield and the outfield. A softball slap of a hit, rocketing right toward the ground. I sat up straighter.

But he was gaining ground quickly: the new Dodger, Mookie Betts. His arms unfurl somehow has his legs sprint, faster, faster, toward the infield. He throws the arm with his glove down toward the green turf, his legs still moving him forward, and somehow the ball plops right into the leather, the force of it throwing him a bit off-balance as he continues to run. "Oh shit!" I yelled on my couch, because on the other side of that gray Dodgers jersey is the even more terrifying right arm, which was plucking the ball from the lattice of the glove and side arming it in a perfect arc to the plate where it arrived ... late. "SAFE!" I yelled, throwing my arms out to the side and almost knocking over my beer bottle. And he was safe. He'd beaten the ball with plenty of time.

Except Betts was walking toward the dugout and several people were morphing their hands around invisible baseballs and pressing them into their ears emphatically, their fingers poking their heads. They wanted a review, and

Atlanta Braves 2021

they got one. The video replay showed that Betts was simply too fast, and Ozuna from the other side of the field, timed his tag incorrectly. He had been several feet off the third base bag when Betts made his catch, and so it was a double play. The inning was over, the kindling doused with water.

I marked it as a baserunning error in my scorebook that I'd started keeping for televised games. It was October, but it didn't feel like it. The players were in Texas in a dome and not wearing jackets and I was on my couch like I had been for (at that point) seven months. What I wanted more than anything was to escape into the play. I wanted to get mad about a slider that hung, to scream about a bunt that popped right up into the pitcher's mitt. I wanted to roll my eyes at a poorly timed throw over to first or a kicked ground ball. My own team (the Washington Nationals) had proven to be a ball of trash rolling downhill since early August, so I decided to pick the good team in the division. I chose Atlanta.

Really, I chose Atlanta because they seemed like they were having fun and I wanted to have fun. On October 8, in the middle of game three of the NLDS, Ronald Acuña Jr. danced his way to the dugout between innings. He held his hands over his head, the ball in one, and shimmied his hips. He spun in a circle at the top of the dugout steps. His teeth are so white and so straight, his smile as bright as the full moon. I forgot for a moment that all of the fans behind him were cardboard cutouts. I smiled back at him from my couch. This was nice. This was what baseball should be. Smile at your teammates, baby, because you're going to the NLCS. In interviews, the Atlanta players said they were dancing in the dugout, that no one could talk because the music was so loud.

I miss that, not being able to talk because it is so loud and everyone is having so much fun. I miss the feeling of a friend's hand cupped around my ear screaming something I still can't hear. I miss being able to celebrate successes, to dance around and spray champagne. Maybe, I thought, the Atlanta players could be my friends. They had something I didn't have, but I'd watched them absolutely ruin the Nationals all year. They were scrappy and smart. They had an energy that felt wholesome but mature. There were no ethical concerns for me about them being underpaid. This would work, I told myself going into the NLCS. I would yet again pick the World Series winning team for my essay in *Baseball Prospectus*. I was the good luck charm. Atlanta was going to WIN. IT. ALL.

You know how it went, but let's relive it anyway. Atlanta defeated the pesky Marlins easily in the Division Series. Three games in a row, and none of them felt like a problem. Only Game 2 even felt close. By the time Acuña Jr. was dancing on the top step of the dugout, an Atlanta win felt as sure as the sun setting. But even though I couldn't focus on the 2020 season at all, I was pretty sure that the Dodgers were a different animal. The Dodgers are shiny. They have players whose names people who don't watch baseball know. They all seem to have necklaces that have been very recently polished. They are Los Angeles. They are tan. They are not so easy to beat.

But Atlanta showed up. Hell yeah. They won Game 1 by four runs: no problem. Then they won Game Two. Lost Game 3, sure, that's fine. Won Game 4. Atlanta was up 3-1. That's a hitter's count. If I were the manager (which I am not) I would tell everyone to calm down. Just play smart, good baseball. Don't do anything stupid, and we'll win this. All we have to do is win one of three games. In fact, I did tell the team this. I told it to them through my television. I was invested now. I applauded.

But as you already know, they didn't play smart, and they didn't play carefully. Immediately after Mookie Betts made his incredible catch and Ozuna made his silly error, Corey Seager came up to bat in the fourth and absolutely smashed a home run. Atlanta was still up 2-1, but something had shifted. They managed to score a run in the eighth, but it never felt hopeful. They lost game five and game six and now the odds were much worse.

By the beginning of Game 7, I could barely see the embers of the team I'd lost in Game 5. But all they had to do was win this one. Win one game. We know, of course, that they did not. We also know that it was the baserunning that got them again. But I would have sworn, before I started writing this piece and looked up the details of that dreaded play, that the baserunning error that soaked the Atlanta team with a firehose and ruined their chances for good came in the eighth or ninth inning. That's how absolutely damning it felt to me.

I remembered it wrong. Memory is a funny thing: superimposing what we know is coming on top of what we know happened. In reality, it was only the fourth inning. The game was tied 2-2. Dodgers relief pitcher Tony Gonsolin led off the fourth inning by walking two batters and giving up an RBI single. There was optimism streaming through the television screen. Maybe my new adopted team could still pull it off. You could see the players sitting up a little bit taller in the dugout.

But the players were distracted. Or maybe they were given bad signals by coaches. With runners on second and third, Justin Turner easily scooped up a rocket of a grounder at third and when he looked up (probably to check on the runners) Dansby Swanson was halfway down the baseline. His head wasn't tucked down. He was running, but it didn't even really seem like he was sprinting. Did he think there was someone on first and he had to? I stood up from my couch with my hands on my head.Turner side-armed it to the plate and began a textbook rundown with the catcher, Swanson shuffling sideways between them down the baseline. Turner stretched, and with Swanson just out of reach dove. He was out. An error. But what's this? Turner hops up from his belly where he landed to his knees, pivots toward third and rockets the ball to the bag. Austin Riley, for some unknown reason, had decided to also make a baserunning error. On the replay, you can see Riley hesitate. He's going toward third, then he's not. He's halfway down the baseline and he chickens out, swallows some bravery and tries again. But he didn't commit soon enough. Riley tucked his legs in a figure

Atlanta Braves 2021

four. He didn't even slide face first into the third out of the inning. 5-2-5-6. The inning was over. Atlanta was up by a run, but they might as well have handed the trophy to the Dodgers then.

I wanted to be mad at him. I wanted so, so badly to be mad. Were this a normal year, I would have been yelling at the television. Who cares that this was a team I adopted for the playoffs! They were making silly, little league mistakes in not one but two games, and giving up a 3-1 lead in the series. It was only the fourth inning. I should have been furious, but optimistic and instead I just felt defeated. It was hard for me to feel mad at Swanson for taking off from the bag when he didn't need to, or at Riley for stealing during a risky rundown. It was hard for me to even feel mad at the coaches. They showed the replay over and over again. Swanson was just out of reach and then Turner dove, laid himself all the way out to brush the pant leg with his glove. It was an incredible effort, and one I could barely believe. Who had that kind of energy in this kind of year, to do something unbelievable?

When I think about the playoffs, I think about those two plays. I'm sure the players do too. The frustration of those plays is that we, the fans, (even me a temporary one) know that the team is better than that. They know it too.

I've thought a lot about those two innings since they happened, replaying the failure in my mind, but that's not really fair. The Atlanta players had a hell of a season. They had a 58.3 win percentage. They won the National League East by four games and crushed the next best team (the Marlins) immediately in the playoffs. Without the errors, they looked good on the field and in the batter's box. Those two mistakes loom large because of their consequences, but they don't define that team. There were five more innings after that baserunning error to come back and win the game. I can't blame them for not being able to mount a comeback. This is a hard year to do anything! In the back of my mind all season I've heard a low but constant hum reminding me that this was just a game in a year where games felt frivolous and unnecessary and dangerous. There will be an asterisk next to this short, weird, awful season for all of history. Those mistakes don't really matter, after all.

This is a year for giving grace where we can afford to. Everyone is working really hard. Everyone is trying their best. Everyone is being given less to work with than a normal year and asked for the same output in return. Sure, there were two mistakes in that series that could have saved Atlanta, but they did have a good season. They had optimism, and dance moves, and only lost to the World Series champions because of mental errors. That's a team that under more normal circumstances, will thrive. And I for one, am really looking forward to watching them again and feeling just a little bit more.

—*Kelsey McKinney is a co-owner at Defector.com.*

Part 2: Player Analysis

PLAYER COMMENTS WITH GRAPHS

Ronald Acuña Jr. LF
Born: 12/18/97 Age: 23 Bats: R Throws: R
Height: 6'0" Weight: 205 Origin: International Free Agent, 2014

YEAR	TEAM	LVL	AGE	PA	R	2B	3B	HR	RBI	BB	K	SB	CS	AVG/OBP/SLG
2018	GWN	AAA	20	101	9	2	0	1	3	11	25	5	1	.211/.297/.267
2018	ATL	MLB	20	487	78	26	4	26	64	45	123	16	5	.293/.366/.552
2019	ATL	MLB	21	715	127	22	2	41	101	76	188	37	9	.280/.365/.518
2020	ATL	MLB	22	202	46	11	0	14	29	38	60	8	1	.250/.406/.581
2021 FS	ATL	MLB	23	600	101	23	3	31	74	72	172	24	8	.268/.365/.508
2021 DC	ATL	MLB	23	623	105	24	3	32	77	75	178	24	9	.268/.365/.508

Comparables: Eric Davis, Kyle Schwarber, Yasiel Puig

    The unfair thing about being Ronald Acuña Jr. is putting up a 6-WARP campaign as a 21-year-old and being expected to be even better the next year. The amazing thing about Acuña is that he was. The Braves' superstar finished in the top 15 in the majors in DRC+ and WARP, nearly doubled his walk rate, was caught just once in nine stolen base attempts, posted a career-high ISO, hard-hit rate and average exit velocity and ranked as one of the fastest runners and better outfielders in the game. The only stumble was a relatively pedestrian .250 batting average, and if that's what you care about, Baseball Prospectus has a wealth of reading material for you.

    In a world without Freddie Freeman, Acuña is Atlanta's MVP, if not the National League's. In a world without fellow second-generation freak Fernando Tatis Jr., Acuña is the easy pick for the best under-25 player in baseball. In a world without Mike Trout, Acuña might be the best player in baseball, full stop. The sky isn't the limit for him; the edge of our known solar system is.

YEAR	TEAM	LVL	AGE	PA	DRC+	BABIP	BRR	FRAA	WARP
2018	GWN	AAA	20	101	78	.281	1.0	LF(18): -3.1, CF(2): -0.6, RF(1): -0.3	-0.5
2018	ATL	MLB	20	487	137	.352	3.1	LF(101): -10.8, CF(13): 1.0, RF(3): 0.3	2.9
2019	ATL	MLB	21	715	129	.337	8.6	CF(100): -3.2, LF(46): 5.0, RF(35): 0.9	6.1
2020	ATL	MLB	22	202	138	.302	1.8	CF(34): 1.2, RF(28): 1.3	1.8
2021 FS	ATL	MLB	23	600	140	.339	1.6	RF 4, CF 0	5.3
2021 DC	ATL	MLB	23	623	140	.339	1.7	RF 4, CF 0	5.1

Ronald Acuña Jr., continued

Batted Ball Distribution

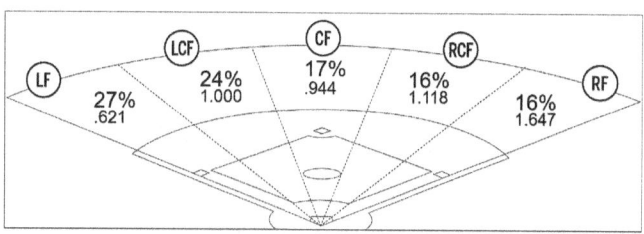

Strike Zone vs LHP   Strike Zone vs RHP

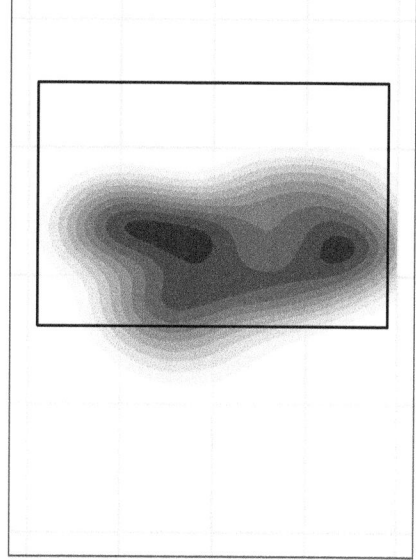

Atlanta Braves 2021

Ehire Adrianza 3B
Born: 08/21/89 Age: 31 Bats: S Throws: R
Height: 6'1" Weight: 195 Origin: International Free Agent, 2006

YEAR	TEAM	LVL	AGE	PA	R	2B	3B	HR	RBI	BB	K	SB	CS	AVG/OBP/SLG
2018	MIN	MLB	28	366	42	23	1	6	39	24	82	5	1	.251/.301/.379
2019	MIN	MLB	29	236	34	8	3	5	22	20	40	0	2	.272/.349/.416
2020	MIN	MLB	30	101	10	7	0	0	3	11	23	1	0	.191/.287/.270
2021 FS	*ATL*	*MLB*	*31*	*600*	*57*	*27*	*2*	*12*	*58*	*51*	*132*	*9*	*4*	*.229/.305/.355*

Comparables: Chris Gomez, Eric Bruntlett, Dale Berra

"The Twins were so unstoppable in 2019 that even Adrianza hit!" may be a terrible one-liner, but it's an adequate snapshot of his recent production.

YEAR	TEAM	LVL	AGE	PA	DRC+	BABIP	BRR	FRAA	WARP
2018	MIN	MLB	28	366	82	.313	0.7	SS(64): -6.1, 3B(28): 0.6, 1B(10): -0.9	0.0
2019	MIN	MLB	29	236	100	.311	-1.2	3B(24): -0.0, SS(24): 1.4, 1B(20): -1.1	0.8
2020	MIN	MLB	30	101	89	.258	0.4	3B(23): -1.0, SS(9): 0.1, 2B(5): -0.4	0.0
2021 FS	*ATL*	*MLB*	*31*	*600*	*83*	*.282*	*0.2*	*SS 0, 3B 0*	*0.0*

Ehire Adrianza, continued

Batted Ball Distribution

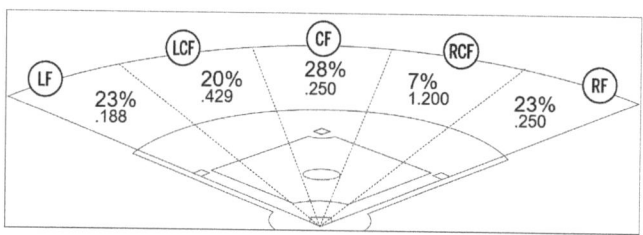

Strike Zone vs LHP

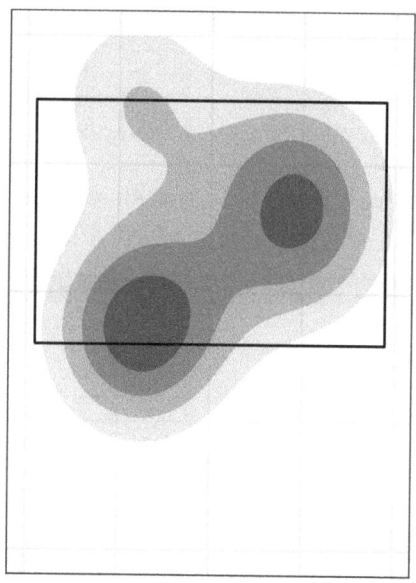

Strike Zone vs RHP

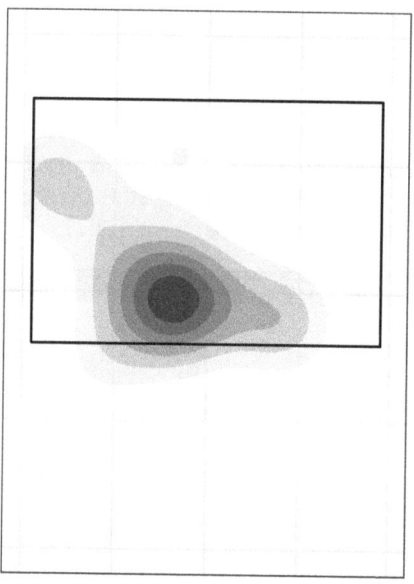

Type	Frequency	Velocity	H Movement	V Movement
● Fastball	94.4%	69.7 [27]	-5.8 [104]	-38.8 [33]
◇ Curveball	5.6%	62.3 [36]	8.5 [104]	-62.9 [68]

Atlanta Braves 2021

Ozzie Albies 2B
Born: 01/07/97 Age: 24 Bats: S Throws: R
Height: 5'8" Weight: 165 Origin: International Free Agent, 2013

YEAR	TEAM	LVL	AGE	PA	R	2B	3B	HR	RBI	BB	K	SB	CS	AVG/OBP/SLG
2018	ATL	MLB	21	684	105	40	5	24	72	36	116	14	3	.261/.305/.452
2019	ATL	MLB	22	702	102	43	8	24	86	54	112	15	4	.295/.352/.500
2020	ATL	MLB	23	124	21	5	0	6	19	5	30	3	1	.271/.306/.466
2021 FS	ATL	MLB	24	600	80	26	5	20	75	42	122	11	4	.260/.317/.438
2021 DC	ATL	MLB	24	574	76	25	5	19	72	41	117	11	3	.260/.317/.438

Comparables: Enrique Hernández, Scooter Gennett, Bobby Grich

A right wrist contusion robbed Albies of about five weeks in an already short season, and hampered him significantly in the few games he played before hitting the injured list in early August. The good news is that, once back, he swung a bat made out of titanium, slashing .338/.372/.581 in September. Before chalking up Albies' overall mediocre season to that balky wrist, though, keep in mind that he took a significant step back in walk rate, going from 7.7 percent in 2019 to a more Rougned Odor-adjacent 4.2 percent this year. Nor can that be blamed entirely on the wrist: Amid that torrid and healthy September, Albies drew a mere three free passes in 78 plate appearances.

Given his average defense and unexceptional base running, Albies' status as a building block for the Braves rests on him figuring out how to take a walk every now and then in addition to his superb power. He did it the year prior, and given that his underlying swing stats didn't nosedive, the safe bet is that Albies finds his way to first more often in 2021.

YEAR	TEAM	LVL	AGE	PA	DRC+	BABIP	BRR	FRAA	WARP
2018	ATL	MLB	21	684	106	.285	5.9	2B(157): 7.0	4.0
2019	ATL	MLB	22	702	119	.325	4.4	2B(158): -0.4	4.4
2020	ATL	MLB	23	124	109	.317	0.6	2B(29): 0.2	0.6
2021 FS	ATL	MLB	24	600	108	.299	0.9	2B 1	2.6
2021 DC	ATL	MLB	24	574	108	.299	0.9	2B 1	2.5

Ozzie Albies, continued

Batted Ball Distribution

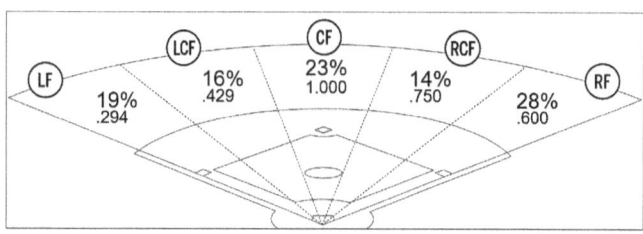

Strike Zone vs LHP   Strike Zone vs RHP

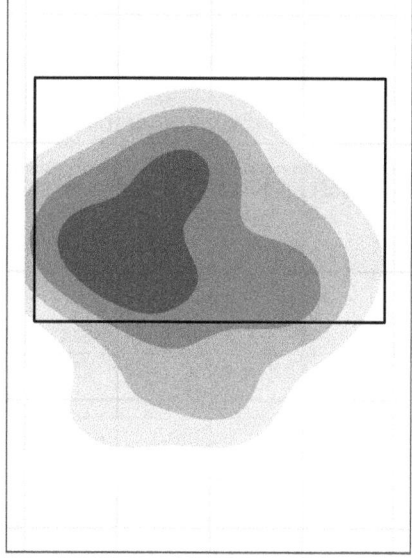

Johan Camargo 3B

Born: 12/13/93   Age: 27   Bats: S   Throws: R
Height: 6'0"   Weight: 195   Origin: International Free Agent, 2010

YEAR	TEAM	LVL	AGE	PA	R	2B	3B	HR	RBI	BB	K	SB	CS	AVG/OBP/SLG
2018	GWN	AAA	24	36	6	2	0	3	7	3	9	0	0	.303/.361/.636
2018	ATL	MLB	24	524	63	27	1	19	76	51	108	1	1	.272/.349/.457
2019	GWN	AAA	25	64	10	6	0	2	15	5	12	0	0	.483/.531/.690
2019	ATL	MLB	25	248	31	12	1	7	32	15	43	1	0	.233/.279/.384
2020	ATL	MLB	26	127	16	8	0	4	9	6	35	0	0	.200/.244/.367
2021 FS	ATL	MLB	27	600	65	25	2	18	69	39	143	0	1	.235/.290/.388
2021 DC	ATL	MLB	27	253	27	10	1	7	29	16	60	0	0	.235/.290/.388

Comparables: Kevin Kouzmanoff, Jim Morrison, Mickey Klutts

It's been a frustrating two years for Camargo, who went from breakout star in 2018 to utility player and Josh Donaldson backup in '19 to... this. His offense disappeared alongside his starting role, and neither reappeared in 2020, as the Braves committed to letting Austin Riley cook at third base, and Camargo wasn't able to steal the job back despite Riley's struggles. Nor did time spent filling in for Albies at second base go any better. The gains he made in 2018 haven't stuck, as Camargo's contact rates and plate discipline have eroded, leaving him decidedly below league-average offensively. His first year of arbitration eligibility arrives in 2021, meaning his paychecks are about to start getting bigger—as will the pressure to prove that 2018 wasn't a fluke.

YEAR	TEAM	LVL	AGE	PA	DRC+	BABIP	BRR	FRAA	WARP
2018	GWN	AAA	24	36	129	.333	0.3	SS(4): -0.5, 3B(3): -0.2, 2B(1): -0.0	0.2
2018	ATL	MLB	24	524	115	.315	-1.6	3B(114): -9.8, SS(18): -1.5, 2B(3): -0.1	1.6
2019	GWN	AAA	25	64	185	.591	-1.9	3B(7): -0.6, SS(4): 0.3, 2B(3): -0.6	0.6
2019	ATL	MLB	25	248	80	.258	0.2	SS(25): 0.5, 3B(18): -0.2, LF(11): 0.3	0.3
2020	ATL	MLB	26	127	80	.247	0.2	2B(21): -1.9, 3B(10): 2.5	0.1
2021 FS	ATL	MLB	27	600	85	.284	-0.7	SS -1, 2B 0	0.3
2021 DC	ATL	MLB	27	253	85	.284	-0.3	SS -1, 2B 0	0.2

Johan Camargo, continued

Batted Ball Distribution

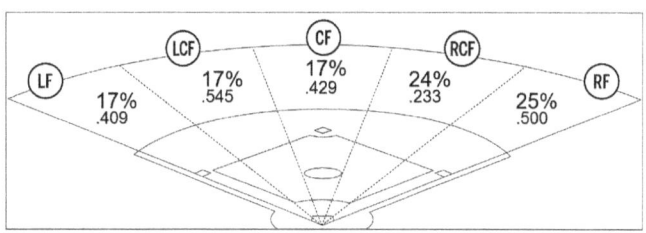

Strike Zone vs LHP   **Strike Zone vs RHP**

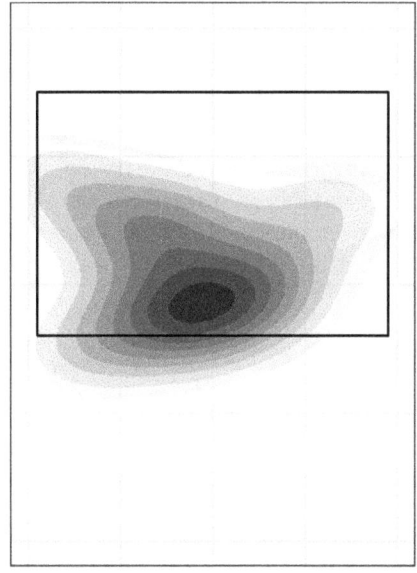
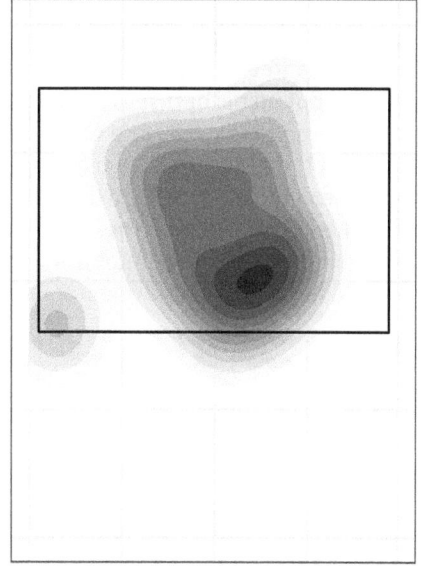

Atlanta Braves 2021

Travis d'Arnaud C
Born: 02/10/89   Age: 32   Bats: R   Throws: R
Height: 6'2"   Weight: 210   Origin: Round 1, 2007 Draft (#37 overall)

YEAR	TEAM	LVL	AGE	PA	R	2B	3B	HR	RBI	BB	K	SB	CS	AVG/OBP/SLG
2018	NYM	MLB	29	16	1	0	0	1	3	1	5	0	0	.200/.250/.400
2019	LAD	MLB	30	1	0	0	0	0	0	0	0	0	0	.000/.000/.000
2019	NYM	MLB	30	25	2	0	0	0	2	2	5	0	0	.087/.160/.087
2019	TB	MLB	30	365	50	16	0	16	67	30	80	0	1	.263/.323/.459
2020	ATL	MLB	31	184	19	8	0	9	34	16	49	1	0	.321/.386/.533
2021 FS	ATL	MLB	32	600	77	25	1	22	81	49	147	0	1	.249/.316/.422
2021 DC	ATL	MLB	32	443	57	18	0	16	60	36	109	0	1	.249/.316/.422

Comparables: Jody Davis, Mike Macfarlane, Ryan Doumit

Perhaps the platonic ideal of a Wilpon-era Mets rage DFA, d'Arnaud split time with three different teams in 2019 (though if you blinked, you missed his stint with the Dodgers), excelled in Tampa Bay and turned that into a two-year, $16 million deal with Atlanta. That was a shrewd investment, as d'Arnaud put up his best season ever at the dish and ranked as one of the better backstops in the league with the glove. Not that there aren't red flags in his profile: His strikeout rate ballooned to 27.2 percent, and despite a drop in contact rates, his BABIP was more peak Ichiro than 31-year-old catcher. A sky-high hard-hit rate of 57.2 percent makes that figure a little more palatable if not probable, but it's unlikely that he can replicate this kind of performance next year.

YEAR	TEAM	P. COUNT	FRM RUNS	BLK RUNS	THRW RUNS	TOT RUNS
2018	NYM	694	1.0	0.1	0.0	1.0
2019	NYM	899	0.2	0.0	0.0	0.2
2019	TB	9708	1.8	-2.4	0.1	-0.6
2020	ATL	5251	3.1	-0.2	0.2	3.1
2021	ATL	13228	8.3	0.0	-0.5	7.8
2021	ATL	13228	8.3	-1.1	-0.5	6.7

YEAR	TEAM	LVL	AGE	PA	DRC+	BABIP	BRR	FRAA	WARP
2018	NYM	MLB	29	16	79	.222	-0.1	C(4): 1.0	0.1
2019	LAD	MLB	30	1	105	.000			0.0
2019	NYM	MLB	30	25	70	.111	0.4	C(9): 0.1	0.1
2019	TB	MLB	30	365	103	.295	0.4	C(76): -2.2, 1B(21): -1.6	1.4
2020	ATL	MLB	31	184	110	.407	-0.8	C(35): -1.0	0.9
2021 FS	ATL	MLB	32	600	104	.301	-0.9	C 7, 1B 0	3.2
2021 DC	ATL	MLB	32	443	104	.301	-0.7	C 7	2.5

Travis d'Arnaud, continued

Batted Ball Distribution

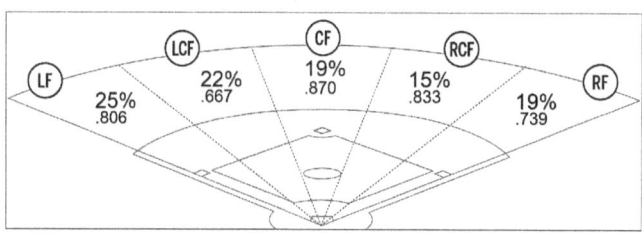

Strike Zone vs LHP   Strike Zone vs RHP

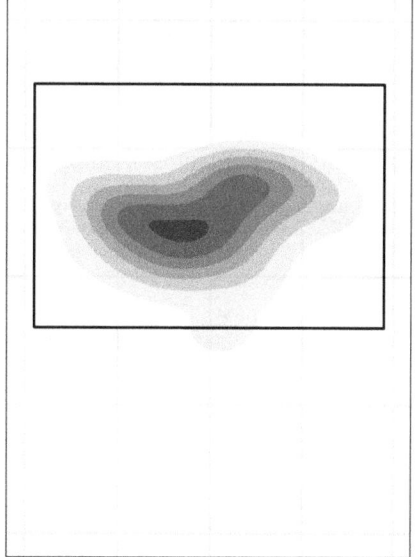

Adam Duvall LF

Born: 09/04/88 Age: 32 Bats: R Throws: R
Height: 6'1" Weight: 215 Origin: Round 11, 2010 Draft (#348 overall)

YEAR	TEAM	LVL	AGE	PA	R	2B	3B	HR	RBI	BB	K	SB	CS	AVG/OBP/SLG
2018	CIN	MLB	29	370	40	19	0	15	61	34	100	2	2	.205/.286/.399
2018	ATL	MLB	29	57	8	1	0	0	0	3	17	0	0	.132/.193/.151
2019	GWN	AAA	30	429	74	20	4	32	93	48	86	1	0	.266/.364/.602
2019	ATL	MLB	30	130	17	4	1	10	19	7	39	0	0	.267/.315/.567
2020	ATL	MLB	31	209	34	8	0	16	33	15	54	0	0	.237/.301/.532
2021 FS	ATL	MLB	32	600	76	27	2	34	92	43	174	4	2	.232/.300/.480
2021 DC	ATL	MLB	32	457	58	20	1	26	70	33	132	3	2	.232/.300/.480

Comparables: Henry Rodriguez, Geoff Jenkins, Bo Jackson

Birthed fully formed from the forehead of Mark Trumbo, Duvall represents a dying breed of hack-happy sluggers who offer virtually nothing else in terms of value. The former All-Star never met a breaking pitch he wouldn't swing at (and over), is fine defensively so long as you don't ask him to do anything beyond the bare minimum, and won't embarrass himself on the basepaths (though he won't win you any games there either). But what Duvall can do is destroy fastballs from those pitchers stupid or stubborn enough to challenge him with heat, and he's a valuable platoon piece as someone who mashes lefties. That should be enough to keep him employed and above league average offensively, despite a toolbox that has only a hammer and a broken tape measure in it. It wasn't, as he found himself one of the autumn's more surprising non-tenders.

YEAR	TEAM	LVL	AGE	PA	DRC+	BABIP	BRR	FRAA	WARP
2018	CIN	MLB	29	370	80	.244	-0.6	LF(89): 6.9, 1B(10): 0.3, 3B(1): -0.0	0.7
2018	ATL	MLB	29	57	82	.194	0.6	LF(12): -0.0, RF(2): -0.0	0.1
2019	GWN	AAA	30	429	134	.261	0.2	LF(51): 4.7, RF(26): 1.5	3.1
2019	ATL	MLB	30	130	104	.306	0.4	LF(31): 1.8, RF(2): -0.5	0.6
2020	ATL	MLB	31	209	121	.240	0.2	LF(45): 0.5, RF(17): -1.6, CF(1): -0.0	0.8
2021 FS	ATL	MLB	32	600	110	.273	-0.3	LF 2, RF 0	2.7
2021 DC	ATL	MLB	32	457	110	.273	-0.2	LF 2, RF 0	1.9

***Adam Duvall**, continued*

Batted Ball Distribution

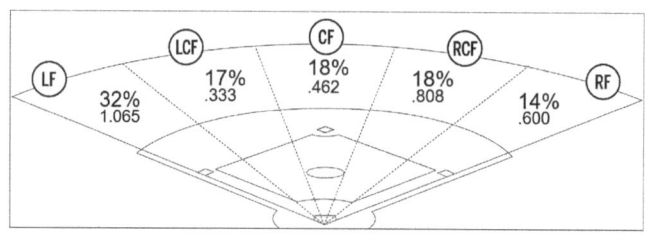

Strike Zone vs LHP   Strike Zone vs RHP

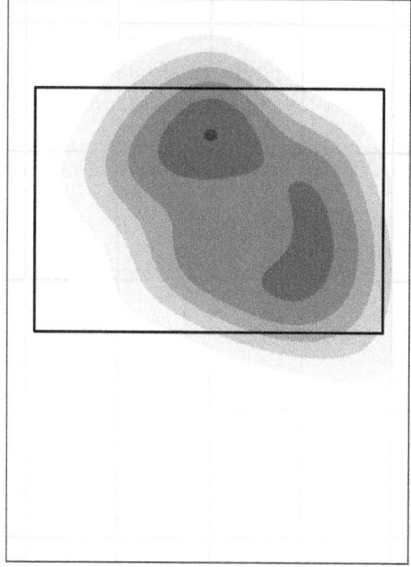

Freddie Freeman 1B

Born: 09/12/89 Age: 31 Bats: L Throws: R
Height: 6'5" Weight: 220 Origin: Round 2, 2007 Draft (#78 overall)

YEAR	TEAM	LVL	AGE	PA	R	2B	3B	HR	RBI	BB	K	SB	CS	AVG/OBP/SLG
2018	ATL	MLB	28	707	94	44	4	23	98	76	132	10	3	.309/.388/.505
2019	ATL	MLB	29	692	113	34	2	38	121	87	127	6	3	.295/.389/.549
2020	ATL	MLB	30	262	51	23	1	13	53	45	37	2	0	.341/.462/.640
2021 FS	ATL	MLB	31	600	99	29	2	29	89	84	116	7	3	.286/.395/.527
2021 DC	ATL	MLB	31	637	105	31	2	31	94	90	123	8	3	.286/.395/.527

Comparables: Mark Teixeira, Adrián González, Harmon Killebrew

A picture may not be worth a thousand words, but in the case of Freeman, a glance at his Brooks Baseball visualizations would tell you the secret to his brilliant 2020: Don't miss the ball when you swing at it, and hit the living crap out of it when you connect. A paragon of consistency, Freeman found new heights by cutting his whiff rate and upping his contact and hard-hit rates (as well as putting the ball on the ground less). That he leveled up at the age of 31 and after 10 years of already excellent results is a testament to the kind of player he is, and a terrifying thought for the rest of the NL East. The future in Atlanta was supposed to be Acuña and Albies. It wasn't supposed to be that plus Freeman morphing into Peak Todd Helton in Coors, and a Coors he can somehow take along on the road.

YEAR	TEAM	LVL	AGE	PA	DRC+	BABIP	BRR	FRAA	WARP
2018	ATL	MLB	28	707	136	.358	-1.7	1B(161): 3.5	4.4
2019	ATL	MLB	29	692	141	.318	0.6	1B(158): -7.5	4.0
2020	ATL	MLB	30	262	172	.366	-2.1	1B(58): -0.2	2.6
2021 FS	ATL	MLB	31	600	153	.318	-0.2	1B 0	5.0
2021 DC	ATL	MLB	31	637	153	.318	-0.2	1B 0	5.3

Freddie Freeman, continued

Batted Ball Distribution

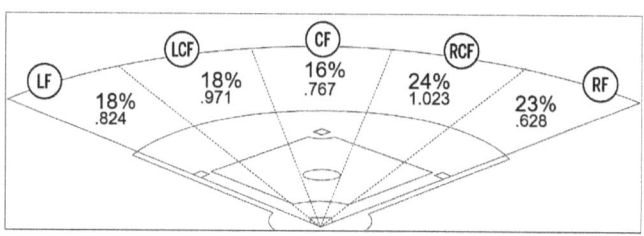

Strike Zone vs LHP   Strike Zone vs RHP

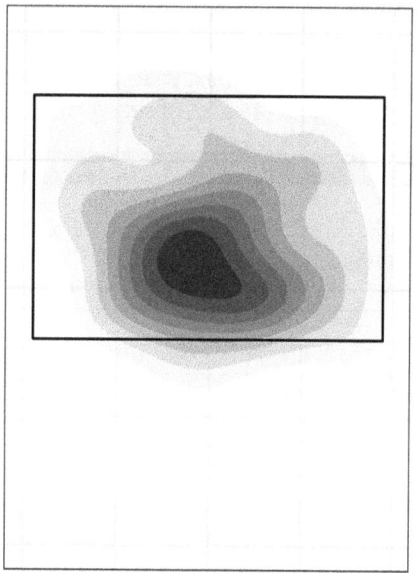

Ender Inciarte CF

Born: 10/29/90 Age: 30 Bats: L Throws: L
Height: 5'11" Weight: 190 Origin: International Free Agent, 2008

YEAR	TEAM	LVL	AGE	PA	R	2B	3B	HR	RBI	BB	K	SB	CS	AVG/OBP/SLG
2018	ATL	MLB	27	660	83	27	6	10	61	49	86	28	14	.265/.325/.380
2019	GWN	AAA	28	30	5	1	0	0	1	4	3	0	1	.231/.333/.269
2019	ATL	MLB	28	230	30	11	2	5	24	26	41	7	1	.246/.343/.397
2020	ATL	MLB	29	131	17	2	1	1	10	12	25	4	1	.190/.262/.250
2021 FS	ATL	MLB	30	600	67	22	3	10	61	48	102	18	8	.251/.316/.365
2021 DC	ATL	MLB	30	370	41	14	2	6	37	29	62	11	5	.251/.316/.365

Comparables: Bobby Tolan, Marquis Grissom, Mike Kingery

Ender's game has long been his glove, and that leather had to speak for the dead in 2020, as his offense slipped to nigh-unplayable levels. Then again, it's hard to imagine any level of defense being good enough to make up for a year where you're 74 percent below league average at the plate, as Inciarte was. It's just fortunate the pitcher wasn't hitting behind him. Already no one's idea of a slugger, his power completely dried up, with just four extra-base hits all season and a hard-hit rate of 6.4 percent. Inciarte can still draw a walk, steal a bag and play the outfield well, making him the quintessential backup outfielder. Unless his bat rebounds next year (a definite possibility, given the small sample size monster that ate a lot of seasons), that's his new ceiling, too.

YEAR	TEAM	LVL	AGE	PA	DRC+	BABIP	BRR	FRAA	WARP
2018	ATL	MLB	27	660	94	.293	2.3	CF(155): 9.6	3.1
2019	GWN	AAA	28	30	85	.261	0.3	CF(5): 0.1	0.1
2019	ATL	MLB	28	230	95	.286	0.4	CF(63): 4.5	1.2
2020	ATL	MLB	29	131	81	.228	-1.1	CF(46): -4.3	-0.5
2021 FS	ATL	MLB	30	600	89	.291	1.4	CF 1	1.3
2021 DC	ATL	MLB	30	370	89	.291	0.9	LF 0, CF 0	0.6

Ender Inciarte, continued

Batted Ball Distribution

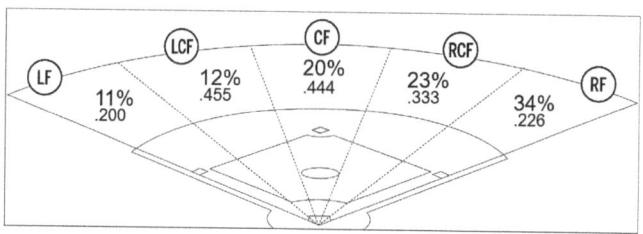

Strike Zone vs LHP   Strike Zone vs RHP

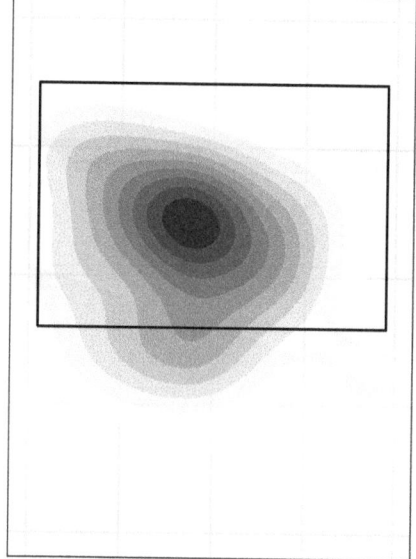

Atlanta Braves 2021

Nick Markakis RF
Born: 11/17/83 Age: 37 Bats: L Throws: L
Height: 6'1" Weight: 210 Origin: Round 1, 2003 Draft (#7 overall)

YEAR	TEAM	LVL	AGE	PA	R	2B	3B	HR	RBI	BB	K	SB	CS	AVG/OBP/SLG
2018	ATL	MLB	34	705	78	43	2	14	93	72	80	1	1	.297/.366/.440
2019	ATL	MLB	35	469	61	25	2	9	62	47	59	2	0	.285/.356/.420
2020	ATL	MLB	36	141	15	15	0	1	15	10	23	0	1	.254/.312/.392
2021 FS	ATL	MLB	37	600	58	29	1	11	58	57	106	1	1	.243/.321/.364
2021 DC	ATL	MLB	37	325	31	16	0	5	31	31	57	0	1	.243/.321/.364

Comparables: Paul O'Neill, George Hendrick, Orlando Merced

Markakis was set to sit out the 2020 season, opting out in early July over the COVID-19 pandemic, only to change course three weeks later and join the Braves after all. That return didn't show up in the box scores, as Markakis posted one of his weakest seasons at the plate in his long career, but despite that, he led the team in starts in right field. The Braves are seemingly content to keep him around until he doesn't want to be there (and then welcome him back when he does), and truthfully, you could do worse in terms of reserve outfield options, particularly when they have the Veteran Intangibles that Markakis does. The trick for the Braves will be to reduce his playing time; at 37, leadership and the occasional start or two every week is just about all Markakis has to offer at this point.

YEAR	TEAM	LVL	AGE	PA	DRC+	BABIP	BRR	FRAA	WARP
2018	ATL	MLB	34	705	116	.318	-1.6	RF(158): 6.9, LF(3): -0.4	3.5
2019	ATL	MLB	35	469	105	.310	-2.8	RF(103): -11.5, LF(9): 3.4	0.4
2020	ATL	MLB	36	141	91	.302	-1.6	RF(29): -2.4, LF(7): 0.7	-0.3
2021 FS	ATL	MLB	37	600	90	.284	-1.0	RF 0, LF 0	0.4
2021 DC	ATL	MLB	37	325	90	.284	-0.5	RF 0, LF 0	0.2

Nick Markakis, continued

Batted Ball Distribution

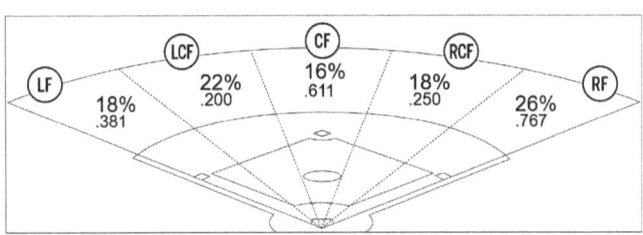

Strike Zone vs LHP   Strike Zone vs RHP

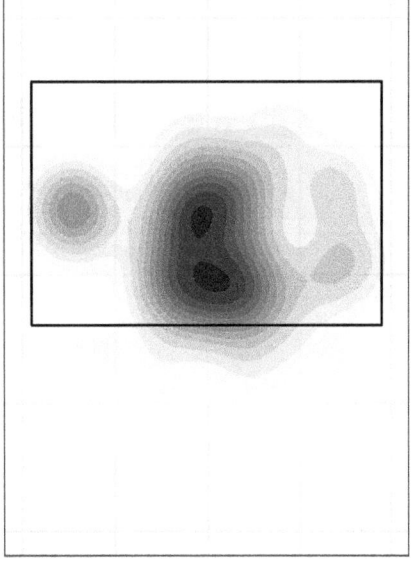

Atlanta Braves 2021

Marcell Ozuna LF
Born: 11/12/90 Age: 30 Bats: R Throws: R
Height: 6'1" Weight: 225 Origin: International Free Agent, 2008

YEAR	TEAM	LVL	AGE	PA	R	2B	3B	HR	RBI	BB	K	SB	CS	AVG/OBP/SLG
2018	STL	MLB	27	628	69	16	2	23	88	38	110	3	0	.280/.325/.433
2019	STL	MLB	28	549	80	23	1	29	89	62	114	12	2	.241/.328/.472
2020	ATL	MLB	29	267	38	14	0	18	56	38	60	0	0	.338/.431/.636
2021 FS	ATL	MLB	30	600	90	24	1	31	97	60	139	3	3	.279/.354/.510
2021 DC	ATL	MLB	30	587	88	24	1	30	95	59	136	3	3	.279/.354/.510

Comparables: Jason Kubel, Rondell White, David Murphy

Like the Pirates used to be with starters on their last legs, the Braves have established themselves as the softest of pillows for sluggers who earned a frosty reception in free agency. Josh Donaldson turned his one-year deal with Atlanta in 2019 into a 5-WARP season and a four-year contract with the Twins. Ozuna is likely to be the next beneficiary of the Braves' single-season signings program, putting up his best season ever as he led the NL in homers, RBI and total bases. Ozuna's putrid defense and mediocre base running suggest that he might not age particularly gracefully. But it's okay to swing through strike one as long as you obliterate strike two, and his 2020 results will net him some long-term security somewhere.

YEAR	TEAM	LVL	AGE	PA	DRC+	BABIP	BRR	FRAA	WARP
2018	STL	MLB	27	628	109	.309	2.6	LF(147): -2.2	2.4
2019	STL	MLB	28	549	111	.257	3.1	LF(129): -11.2	1.5
2020	ATL	MLB	29	267	151	.391	-0.2	LF(19): 3.1, RF(2): -0.2	2.4
2021 FS	ATL	MLB	30	600	136	.321	-0.5	LF 0, RF 0	4.3
2021 DC	ATL	MLB	30	587	136	.321	-0.4	LF 0	3.7

Marcell Ozuna, continued

Batted Ball Distribution

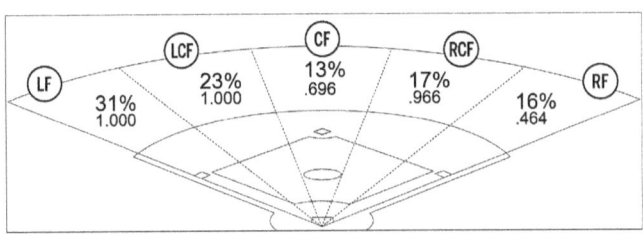

Strike Zone vs LHP   **Strike Zone vs RHP**

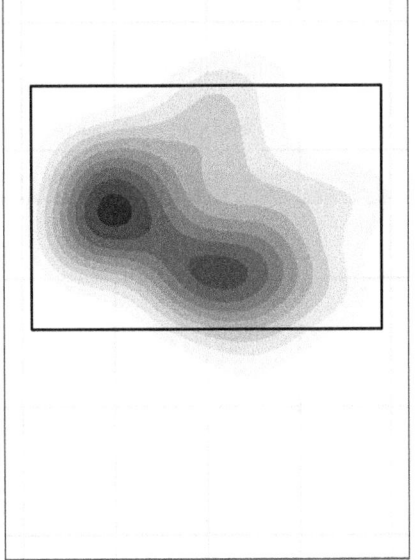

Braves Player Analysis - 35

Atlanta Braves 2021

Austin Riley 3B

Born: 04/02/97   Age: 24   Bats: R   Throws: R
Height: 6'3"   Weight: 240   Origin: Round 1, 2015 Draft (#41 overall)

YEAR	TEAM	LVL	AGE	PA	R	2B	3B	HR	RBI	BB	K	SB	CS	AVG/OBP/SLG
2018	MIS	AA	21	109	17	10	3	6	20	8	28	0	0	.333/.394/.677
2018	GWN	AAA	21	324	41	17	0	12	47	26	95	1	0	.282/.346/.464
2019	GWN	AAA	22	194	39	13	0	15	41	20	39	0	0	.293/.366/.626
2019	ATL	MLB	22	297	41	11	1	18	49	16	108	0	2	.226/.279/.471
2020	ATL	MLB	23	206	24	7	1	8	27	16	49	0	0	.239/.301/.415
2021 FS	ATL	MLB	24	600	75	24	2	27	85	46	177	0	1	.239/.303/.443
2021 DC	ATL	MLB	24	479	60	19	1	21	68	36	141	0	1	.239/.303/.443

Comparables: Pete Incaviglia, Frank Howard, Pat Burrell

To get a sense of the kind of hitter Riley is, here are his monthly splits in 2020 by OPS: .371 (July), .875 (August), .669 (September), .489 (October). Tiny sample sizes abound in those cutoffs, but the point is that Atlanta's young third baseman is as streaky as they come. Not that this should come as a surprise, blessed as Riley is with prodigious power yet cursed at the same time with the plate discipline of a blindfolded Mark Reynolds. On the plus side, he did substantially cut down his strikeout rate from 2019 to '20; on the less positive side, it's still triple his anemic walk rate. At age 23, he remains a work in progress both with the bat and the glove, and one who needs to take a significant step forward with both in 2021 to remain part of Atlanta's long-term plans.

YEAR	TEAM	LVL	AGE	PA	DRC+	BABIP	BRR	FRAA	WARP
2018	MIS	AA	21	109	175	.415	1.0	3B(27): 1.2	1.3
2018	GWN	AAA	21	324	122	.374	1.1	3B(71): -0.3	1.5
2019	GWN	AAA	22	194	138	.300	0.2	3B(30): -0.9, LF(7): -0.8, 1B(4): 0.2	1.3
2019	ATL	MLB	22	297	89	.293	-0.4	LF(58): 2.0, 1B(6): -0.8, 3B(5): -0.3	0.4
2020	ATL	MLB	23	206	91	.280	-0.2	3B(46): 1.2, 1B(4): 0.3, LF(4): -0.0	0.3
2021 FS	ATL	MLB	24	600	104	.299	-0.8	3B 0, 1B 0	1.5
2021 DC	ATL	MLB	24	479	104	.299	-0.6	3B 0	1.1

Austin Riley, continued

Batted Ball Distribution

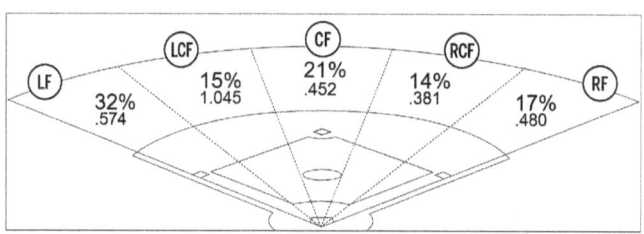

Strike Zone vs LHP   **Strike Zone vs RHP**

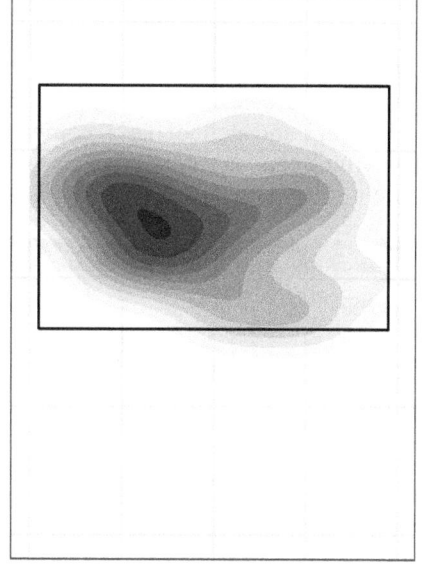

Atlanta Braves 2021

Dansby Swanson SS
Born: 02/11/94   Age: 27   Bats: R   Throws: R
Height: 6'1"   Weight: 190   Origin: Round 1, 2015 Draft (#1 overall)

YEAR	TEAM	LVL	AGE	PA	R	2B	3B	HR	RBI	BB	K	SB	CS	AVG/OBP/SLG
2018	ATL	MLB	24	533	51	25	4	14	59	44	122	10	4	.238/.304/.395
2019	ATL	MLB	25	545	77	26	3	17	65	51	124	10	5	.251/.325/.422
2020	ATL	MLB	26	264	49	15	0	10	35	22	71	5	0	.274/.345/.464
2021 FS	ATL	MLB	27	600	76	25	2	18	70	57	156	7	3	.239/.317/.399
2021 DC	ATL	MLB	27	588	74	25	2	17	69	56	153	7	3	.239/.317/.399

Comparables: Jose Valentin, Julio Lugo, Alex Gonzalez

Following a sophomore slump that stretched all the way through his senior year, Swanson looked like nothing more than a nice head of hair and disarmingly attractive face attached to a solid glove, a noodle bat and a name that's exceedingly fun to say in a syrupy, deep Southern accent. Yet the Man Who Would Be Waffle House King (and favorite son of Cobb County dads who tuck their golf shirts into their khaki shorts) showed his no. 1 pick bona fides in 2020, with a career-best DRC+ and what likely would've been a 3-WARP campaign over a full year. The concern is that Swanson built that success on a foundation of sand, as none of his swing or contact rates took any noticeable tick in the right direction; in fact, his whiffs went up, as did his strikeouts. A high BABIP papered over those issues, as did the numbers he put up on fastballs (a .588 slugging percentage and eight of his 10 homers), though he continued to flail against everything else. What gains he made seem easily reversible if they exist at all; 2021 will be in many ways a make-or-break season for the Georgia native.

YEAR	TEAM	LVL	AGE	PA	DRC+	BABIP	BRR	FRAA	WARP
2018	ATL	MLB	24	533	90	.290	0.9	SS(136): 5.4	2.5
2019	ATL	MLB	25	545	97	.300	1.6	SS(126): 1.3	2.7
2020	ATL	MLB	26	264	107	.350	2.1	SS(60): -2.3	1.0
2021 FS	ATL	MLB	27	600	99	.301	0.0	SS 1	1.9
2021 DC	ATL	MLB	27	588	99	.301	0.0	SS 1	1.8

Dansby Swanson, continued

Batted Ball Distribution

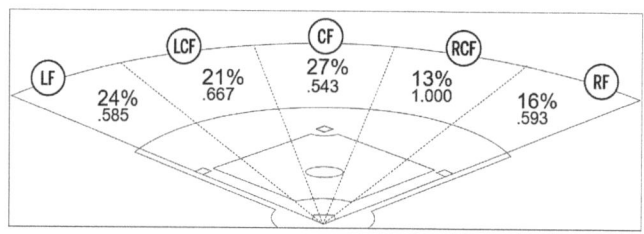

Strike Zone vs LHP   Strike Zone vs RHP

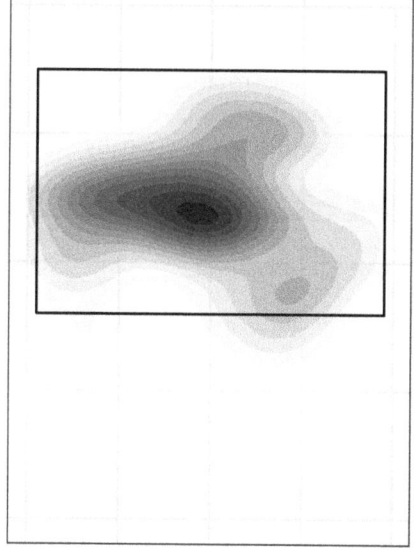

Ian Anderson RHP

Born: 05/02/98 Age: 23 Bats: R Throws: R
Height: 6'3" Weight: 170 Origin: Round 1, 2016 Draft (#3 overall)

YEAR	TEAM	LVL	AGE	W	L	SV	G	GS	IP	H	HR	BB/9	K/9	K	GB%	BABIP
2018	FLO	HI-A	20	2	6	0	20	20	100	73	2	3.6	10.6	118	44.9%	.285
2018	MIS	AA	20	2	1	0	4	4	19^1	14	0	4.2	11.2	24	43.5%	.311
2019	MIS	AA	21	7	5	0	21	21	111	82	8	3.8	11.9	147	44.4%	.290
2019	GWN	AAA	21	1	2	0	5	5	24^2	23	5	6.6	9.1	25	37.1%	.277
2020	ATL	MLB	22	3	2	0	6	6	32^1	21	1	3.9	11.4	41	53.1%	.250
2021 FS	ATL	MLB	23	9	8	0	26	26	150	132	19	4.3	10.2	169	45.7%	.293
2021 DC	ATL	MLB	23	9	8	0	27	25	139.7	123	17	4.3	10.2	158	45.7%	.293

Comparables: Archie Bradley, Henry Owens, Dustin May

Tasked with helping save a Braves rotation taking on more water than the *Titanic*, the 22-year-old Anderson did just that, shouldering the team by giving up two runs in four postseason starts. Not bad for a rookie just four years removed from facing 16-year-olds in upstate New York. Anderson marries quality velocity with a devastating changeup that batters simply can't touch: They hit .104 against it with a whiff rate of 39.8 percent. The next step for him is tightening up his control and continuing to refine his curveball, which was more of a show-me pitch than a showstopper in his debut season. Still, he's already displayed a mid-rotation floor with ace upside and is the latest victory for Atlanta's impressive player development system (and the team cloning machine that's set exclusively to "Dansby Swanson").

YEAR	TEAM	LVL	AGE	WHIP	ERA	DRA-	WARP	MPH	FB%	WHF	CSP
2018	FLO	HI-A	20	1.13	2.52	68	2.3				
2018	MIS	AA	20	1.19	2.33	67	0.5				
2019	MIS	AA	21	1.16	2.68	78	1.6				
2019	GWN	AAA	21	1.66	6.57	100	0.4				
2020	ATL	MLB	22	1.08	1.95	65	0.9	95.9	48.5%	29.0%	
2021 FS	ATL	MLB	23	1.36	3.94	93	2.0	95.9	48.5%	29.0%	46.4%
2021 DC	ATL	MLB	23	1.36	3.94	93	1.8	95.9	48.5%	29.0%	46.4%

Ian Anderson, continued

Pitch Shape vs LHH

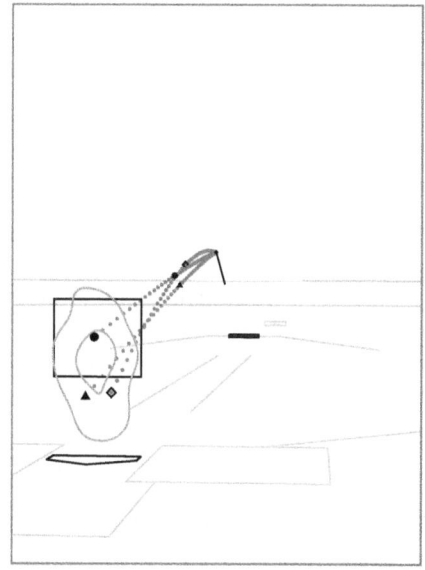

Pitch Shape vs RHH

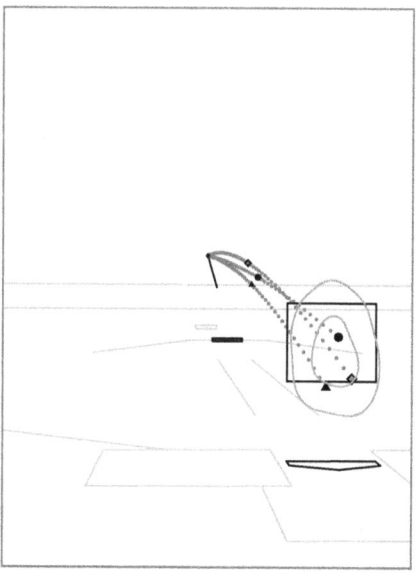

Type	Frequency	Velocity	H Movement	V Movement
● Fastball	48.2%	94.3 [105]	-4.2 [112]	-11.3 [111]
▲ Changeup	30.6%	87.6 [110]	-9 [114]	-21.1 [118]
◇ Curveball	20.8%	80.3 [106]	1.4 [75]	-43.8 [110]

Atlanta Braves 2021

Grant Dayton LHP
Born: 11/25/87 Age: 33 Bats: L Throws: L
Height: 6'2" Weight: 210 Origin: Round 11, 2010 Draft (#347 overall)

YEAR	TEAM	LVL	AGE	W	L	SV	G	GS	IP	H	HR	BB/9	K/9	K	GB%	BABIP
2019	GWN	AAA	31	0	1	0	22	0	26²	20	6	1.4	13.8	41	38.6%	.280
2019	ATL	MLB	31	0	1	0	14	0	12	12	4	3.0	10.5	14	39.4%	.276
2020	ATL	MLB	32	2	1	0	18	0	27¹	22	4	3.6	10.5	32	26.0%	.265
2021 FS	ATL	MLB	33	3	2	0	57	0	50	38	7	3.0	10.6	58	32.6%	.262
2021 DC	ATL	MLB	33	2	2	0	45	0	48.7	37	6	3.0	10.6	57	32.6%	.262

Comparables: Justin Miller, Oliver Drake, Ryan Tepera

A broken toe cost Dayton a bigger role in Atlanta's bullpen in 2019, but given a new opportunity in 2020, he was one of Brian Snitker's better southpaw options, viciously handcuffing left-handed batters to the tune of a .398 OPS. That lefty-on-lefty success was about all Dayton had going for him, though. Right-handed hitters crushed him, his velocity is subpar and his stuff grades out as average. Despite throwing his curveball more often and with more break, the results were mediocre at best, with a .289 batting average against and a 22.7 percent whiff rate. Middle relief is almost certainly his ceiling, and he should be personally lobbying Rob Manfred to undo the three-batter minimum.

YEAR	TEAM	LVL	AGE	WHIP	ERA	DRA-	WARP	MPH	FB%	WHF	CSP
2019	GWN	AAA	31	0.90	3.04	51	1.0				
2019	ATL	MLB	31	1.33	3.00	82	0.2	92.5	76.5%	26.2%	
2020	ATL	MLB	32	1.21	2.30	107	0.1	92.0	62.9%	29.6%	
2021 FS	ATL	MLB	33	1.09	2.83	72	1.0	92.1	65.8%	28.9%	43.9%
2021 DC	ATL	MLB	33	1.09	2.83	72	1.0	92.1	65.8%	28.9%	43.9%

Grant Dayton, continued

Pitch Shape vs LHH

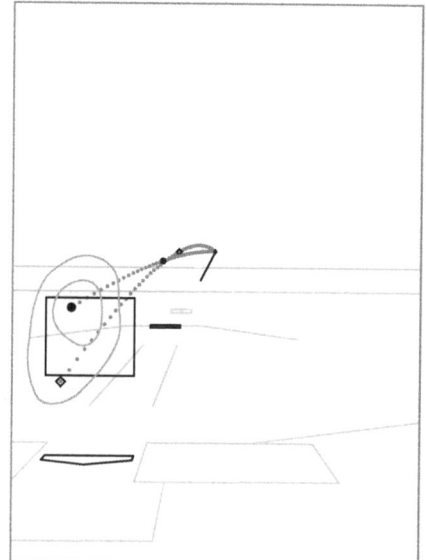

Pitch Shape vs RHH

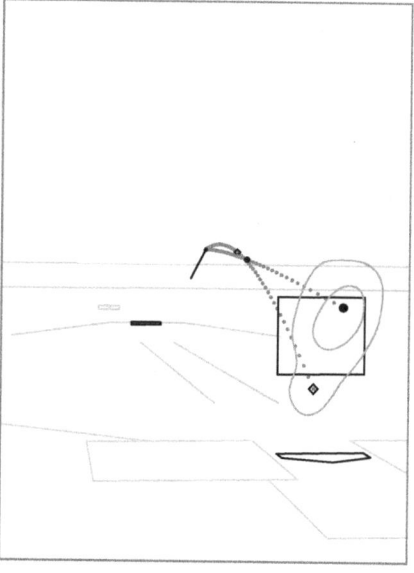

Type	Frequency	Velocity	H Movement	V Movement
● Fastball	62.0%	90.8 [94]	7.6 [96]	-14 [103]
◇ Curveball	36.2%	76 [90]	-5.5 [92]	-54.6 [86]

Atlanta Braves 2021

Robbie Erlin   LHP
Born: 10/08/90   Age: 30   Bats: R   Throws: L
Height: 5'11"   Weight: 200   Origin: Round 3, 2009 Draft (#93 overall)

YEAR	TEAM	LVL	AGE	W	L	SV	G	GS	IP	H	HR	BB/9	K/9	K	GB%	BABIP
2018	SD	MLB	27	4	7	0	39	12	109	112	12	1.0	7.3	88	46.3%	.309
2019	ELP	AAA	28	0	1	1	10	0	15^1	26	2	1.2	8.2	14	47.3%	.462
2019	SD	MLB	28	0	1	0	37	1	55^1	72	6	2.4	8.5	52	44.8%	.375
2020	ATL	MLB	29	0	0	0	9	5	26^2	33	8	2.4	8.4	25	28.4%	.312
2021 FS	ATL	MLB	30	2	2	0	57	0	50	50	7	2.1	7.9	44	40.1%	.296

Comparables: Kevin Gausman, Erasmo Ramírez, Alex Wood

A good sign of how badly the Braves' rotation was torn apart by injuries is that they claimed Robbie Erlin off waivers after he'd been designated for assignment by the *Pirates*. One team's trash didn't turn into another's treasure, as the veteran lefty was lit up over five brutal starts and subsequently let go in mid-September. The Pirates did not retrieve him.

YEAR	TEAM	LVL	AGE	WHIP	ERA	DRA-	WARP	MPH	FB%	WHF	CSP
2018	SD	MLB	27	1.14	4.21	68	2.6	91.8	59.2%	20.9%	
2019	ELP	AAA	28	1.83	8.80	119	0.1				
2019	SD	MLB	28	1.57	5.37	106	0.1	91.9	50.7%	23.6%	
2020	ATL	MLB	29	1.50	8.10	156	-0.6	91.1	56.6%	19.3%	
2021 FS	ATL	MLB	30	1.26	3.99	98	0.3	91.6	55.1%	21.5%	48.7%

Robbie Erlin, continued

Pitch Shape vs LHH

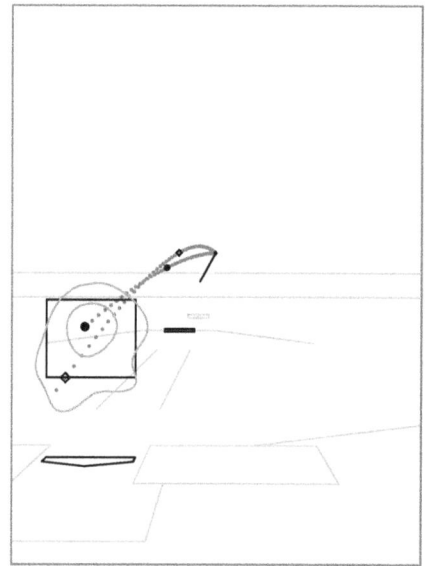

Pitch Shape vs RHH

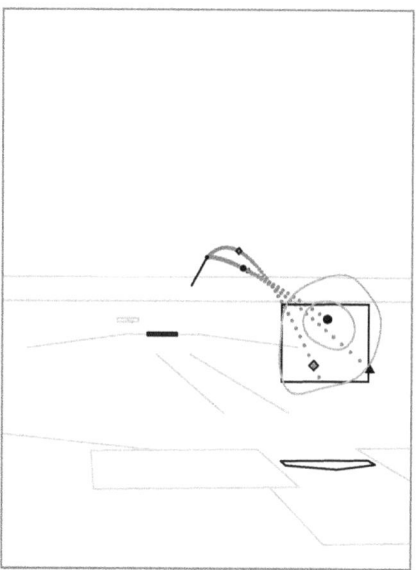

Type	Frequency	Velocity	H Movement	V Movement
● Fastball	56.1%	89.6 [90]	7.5 [96]	-15.6 [99]
▲ Changeup	15.9%	83.1 [92]	8.8 [116]	-27.9 [99]
◇ Curveball	27.1%	76.2 [90]	-6.3 [95]	-56.7 [82]

Max Fried LHP

Born: 01/18/94   Age: 27   Bats: L   Throws: L
Height: 6'4"   Weight: 190   Origin: Round 1, 2012 Draft (#7 overall)

YEAR	TEAM	LVL	AGE	W	L	SV	G	GS	IP	H	HR	BB/9	K/9	K	GB%	BABIP
2018	MIS	AA	24	1	0	0	2	2	11^1	4	0	3.2	12.7	16	66.7%	.190
2018	GWN	AAA	24	2	6	0	13	13	66^1	66	4	4.1	9.6	71	56.2%	.346
2018	ATL	MLB	24	1	4	0	14	5	33^2	26	3	5.3	11.8	44	50.0%	.324
2019	ATL	MLB	25	17	6	0	33	30	165^2	174	21	2.6	9.4	173	52.8%	.338
2020	ATL	MLB	26	7	0	0	11	11	56	42	2	3.1	8.0	50	52.3%	.268
2021 FS	ATL	MLB	27	9	8	0	26	26	150	140	17	3.6	9.4	157	52.7%	.302
2021 DC	ATL	MLB	27	10	8	0	27	27	156.7	147	18	3.6	9.4	164	52.7%	.302

Comparables: Anthony Banda, Chase De Jong, Eduardo Rodriguez

Fun fact: Fried's middle name is Dorian, which suggests that there's a ghastly portrait of him somewhere in the bowels of an abandoned Turner Field getting visibly older and uglier with every curveball he flicks. Set to turn 27 in January, Fried is somehow the grizzled veteran in Atlanta's rotation of baby geniuses, despite having thrown fewer innings in his career than Charlie Hough did in 1987. He was also one of the few reliable presences in a battered rotation, chipping in five or more innings each turn with regularity. Fried doesn't get the whiffs you want to see in a frontline pitcher thanks to his pedestrian fastball, but he's a master at avoiding hard contact and getting weak ground balls, and that curve remains a work of art.

YEAR	TEAM	LVL	AGE	WHIP	ERA	DRA-	WARP	MPH	FB%	WHF	CSP
2018	MIS	AA	24	0.71	0.00	69	0.3				
2018	GWN	AAA	24	1.45	4.61	88	0.9				
2018	ATL	MLB	24	1.37	2.94	73	0.7	96.3	58.7%	34.3%	
2019	ATL	MLB	25	1.33	4.02	70	4.2	96.3	56.9%	26.0%	
2020	ATL	MLB	26	1.09	2.25	81	1.1	95.6	51.9%	25.6%	
2021 FS	ATL	MLB	27	1.34	3.93	93	2.0	96.1	55.5%	26.4%	48.0%
2021 DC	ATL	MLB	27	1.34	3.93	93	2.0	96.1	55.5%	26.4%	48.0%

Max Fried, continued

Pitch Shape vs LHH

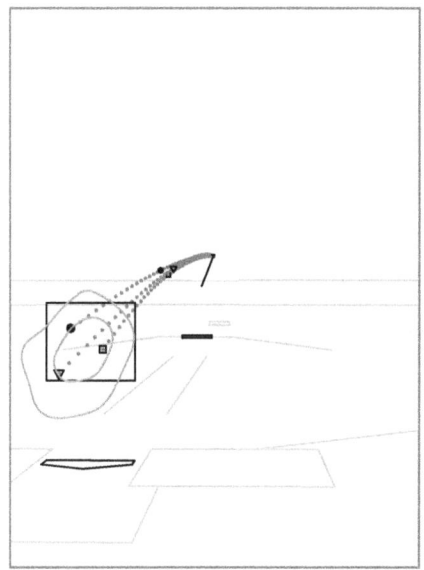

Pitch Shape vs RHH

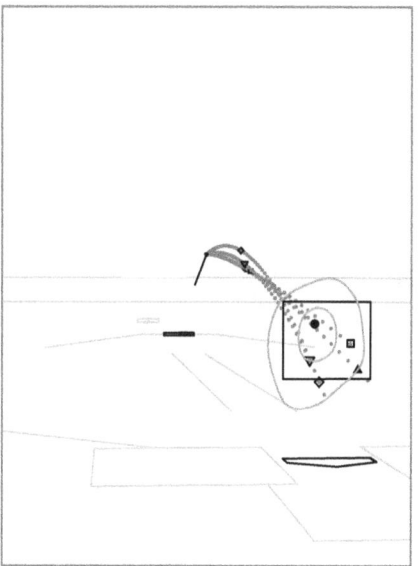

Type	Frequency	Velocity	H Movement	V Movement
● Fastball	40.6%	93.3 [102]	1.1 [127]	-17.8 [93]
□ Sinker	11.2%	92.5 [101]	9.5 [126]	-20.5 [100]
▲ Changeup	5.0%	83.4 [93]	9.2 [113]	-30.4 [92]
▽ Slider	20.6%	84.2 [101]	-10.9 [121]	-34.8 [97]
◇ Curveball	22.5%	74.5 [84]	-9.7 [109]	-61 [72]

Shane Greene RHP

Born: 11/17/88 Age: 32 Bats: R Throws: R
Height: 6'4" Weight: 200 Origin: Round 15, 2009 Draft (#465 overall)

YEAR	TEAM	LVL	AGE	W	L	SV	G	GS	IP	H	HR	BB/9	K/9	K	GB%	BABIP
2018	DET	MLB	29	4	6	32	66	0	63^1	68	12	2.7	9.2	65	41.1%	.311
2019	ATL	MLB	30	0	1	1	27	0	24^2	25	3	1.8	7.7	21	38.4%	.314
2019	DET	MLB	30	0	2	22	38	0	38	21	5	2.8	10.2	43	52.6%	.180
2020	ATL	MLB	31	1	0	0	28	0	27^2	22	2	2.9	6.8	21	42.9%	.270
2021 FS	ATL	MLB	32	2	2	0	57	0	50	46	7	3.0	8.6	47	44.2%	.284

Comparables: Alex Colomé, Andrew Miller, Brandon Workman

No longer a closer and never blessed with the premium velocity that most closers have, Greene appears to have embraced his transition into middle relief by abandoning the results that made him a ninth-inning option in the first place. His strikeout rate of 19.3 percent landed him in the bottom fifth among qualified relievers, and his swinging-strike rate was a mere 7.5 percent. That decline in whiffs plus his age as he reaches free agency is like stripping the tires off of a used car, but Greene succeeded anyway thanks to a changeup he infrequently fiddled with in 2019 but used routinely in '20. That pitch was a winner: a .167 batting average against, a .227 expected wOBA and a 28 percent whiff rate. That'll help him keep hard contact away and, along with his ability to stymie righties, secure a spot as a sixth- or seventh-inning guy—his spiritual home all this time, as it turns out.

YEAR	TEAM	LVL	AGE	WHIP	ERA	DRA-	WARP	MPH	FB%	WHF	CSP
2018	DET	MLB	29	1.37	5.12	87	0.7	96.0	50.8%	21.9%	
2019	ATL	MLB	30	1.22	4.01	89	0.3	93.6	43.3%	25.8%	
2019	DET	MLB	30	0.87	1.18	65	0.9	94.4	49.4%	26.6%	
2020	ATL	MLB	31	1.12	2.60	95	0.3	93.5	39.4%	20.0%	
2021 FS	ATL	MLB	32	1.27	3.86	94	0.4	94.5	45.8%	23.3%	50.1%

Shane Greene, continued

Pitch Shape vs LHH

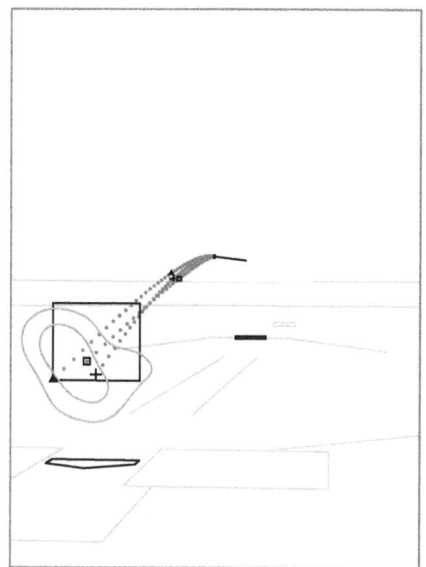

Pitch Shape vs RHH

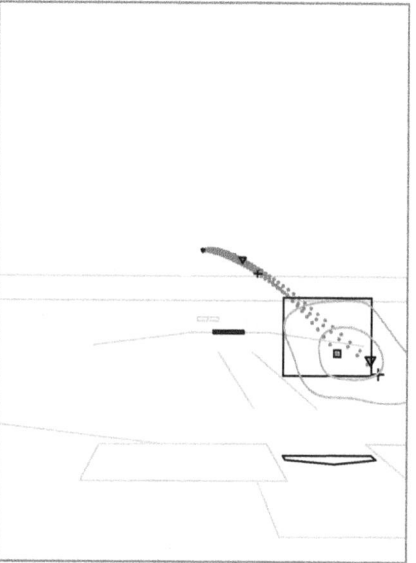

Type	Frequency	Velocity	H Movement	V Movement
☐ Sinker	37.6%	92.2 [99]	-14.3 [91]	-21.5 [97]
+ Cutter	25.4%	87.5 [95]	4.5 [117]	-24.6 [98]
▲ Changeup	13.2%	86.2 [104]	-11.6 [101]	-33.5 [84]
▽ Slider	21.4%	80.7 [86]	13.2 [130]	-33.9 [99]

Luke Jackson RHP

Born: 08/24/91 Age: 29 Bats: R Throws: R
Height: 6'2" Weight: 210 Origin: Round 1, 2010 Draft (#45 overall)

YEAR	TEAM	LVL	AGE	W	L	SV	G	GS	IP	H	HR	BB/9	K/9	K	GB%	BABIP
2018	GWN	AAA	26	2	1	0	10	1	21^1	11	0	4.2	14.3	34	42.1%	.289
2018	ATL	MLB	26	1	2	1	35	0	40^2	41	3	4.6	10.2	46	47.8%	.342
2019	ATL	MLB	27	9	2	18	70	0	72^2	76	10	3.2	13.1	106	59.1%	.388
2020	ATL	MLB	28	2	0	0	19	0	26^1	39	2	4.4	6.8	20	61.9%	.389
2021 FS	ATL	MLB	29	2	2	0	57	0	50	46	5	3.9	9.4	52	53.6%	.301
2021 DC	ATL	MLB	29	2	2	0	45	0	48.7	45	5	3.9	9.4	51	53.6%	.301

Comparables: Austin Brice, Kevin McCarthy, Michael Lorenzen

Jackson has both the name and appearance of a guy who writes mildly popular songs about how relationships are like busting horses or fixing tractors that slot somewhere in the 20s on Billboard's country charts. Given how badly things went last season, he may want to consider picking up a six-string and seeing what he can eke out of it. An out-of-nowhere relief ace for the first half of 2019, Jackson slammed back to earth after the beginning of July and continued drilling through the soil in 2020, with equally huge drops in strikeout rate and fastball velocity. He can still get the ground balls, but that's it; that outstanding whiff rate that elevated his game in 2019 looks like the outlier. He's a mediocre middle reliever until proven otherwise, or until he teams up with Brooks and Dunn to record a new Braves team anthem.

YEAR	TEAM	LVL	AGE	WHIP	ERA	DRA-	WARP	MPH	FB%	WHF	CSP
2018	GWN	AAA	26	0.98	1.69	38	0.8				
2018	ATL	MLB	26	1.52	4.43	129	-0.4	96.1	41.7%	25.2%	
2019	ATL	MLB	27	1.40	3.84	65	1.7	97.4	37.9%	36.8%	
2020	ATL	MLB	28	1.97	6.84	84	0.5	95.8	37.4%	23.2%	
2021 FS	ATL	MLB	29	1.35	3.81	91	0.5	96.7	38.3%	30.7%	42.4%
2021 DC	ATL	MLB	29	1.35	3.81	91	0.5	96.7	38.3%	30.7%	42.4%

Luke Jackson, *continued*

Pitch Shape vs LHH

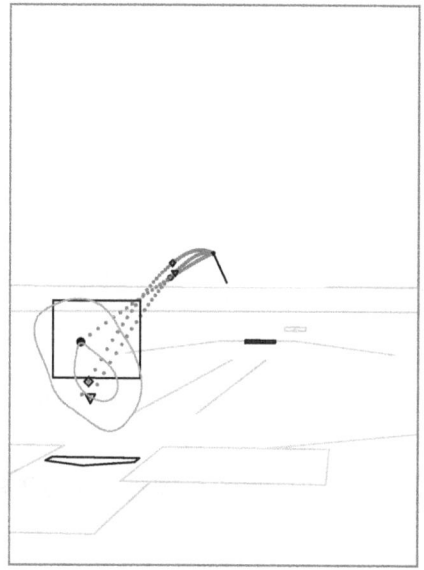

Pitch Shape vs RHH

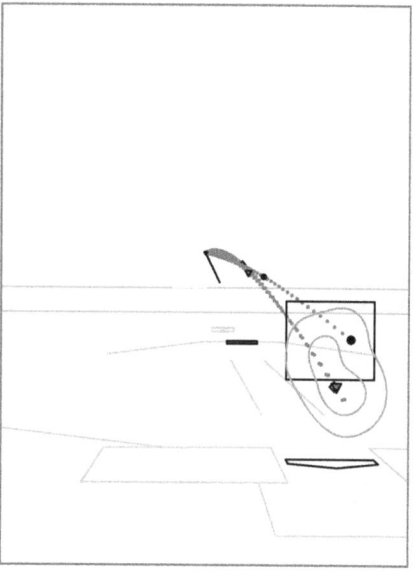

Type	Frequency	Velocity	H Movement	V Movement
● Fastball	36.0%	94.5 [106]	-7.1 [98]	-11.2 [111]
▽ Slider	41.5%	86.7 [112]	1.8 [87]	-37.4 [89]
◇ Curveball	21.1%	83.6 [119]	5.6 [92]	-46.6 [104]

Atlanta Braves 2021

Nate Jones   RHP
Born: 01/28/86   Age: 35   Bats: R   Throws: R
Height: 6'5"   Weight: 230   Origin: Round 5, 2007 Draft (#179 overall)

YEAR	TEAM	LVL	AGE	W	L	SV	G	GS	IP	H	HR	BB/9	K/9	K	GB%	BABIP
2018	CHW	MLB	32	2	2	5	33	0	30	28	4	4.5	9.6	32	40.2%	.293
2019	CHW	MLB	33	0	1	1	13	0	10^1	10	2	6.1	8.7	10	51.7%	.296
2020	CIN	MLB	34	0	1	0	21	0	18^2	25	5	2.9	11.1	23	40.0%	.400
2021 FS	ATL	MLB	35	2	2	0	57	0	50	46	8	3.4	9.3	51	42.7%	.290

Comparables: Brad Brach, Steve Cishek, Tyler Clippard

"Make 'em hit ya. Trust your stuff. Challenge 'em. Throw it over the plate." Sometimes listening to trusty pitching coach chestnuts like those can lead to pitchers posting greatly improved walk and strikeout rates, like Jones did last year. The downside is that letting your fastball sublet a studio in the heart of the zone can also lead to lots of hard contact, and the location heat map of Jones' mid-90s sinker last year looks like three eggs frying in the middle of an oversized skillet. Hitters laid off his slider and tattooed his two-seamer, spraying line drives all over the yard and over the fence. Jones still has stuff that can survive in a big-league bullpen, but only if he can remember how to work the edges.

YEAR	TEAM	LVL	AGE	WHIP	ERA	DRA-	WARP	MPH	FB%	WHF	CSP
2018	CHW	MLB	32	1.43	3.00	101	0.1	98.6	64.7%	30.7%	
2019	CHW	MLB	33	1.65	3.48	110	0.0	96.1	58.3%	25.9%	
2020	CIN	MLB	34	1.66	6.27	97	0.2	97.4	53.5%	33.0%	
2021 FS	ATL	MLB	35	1.31	4.18	95	0.4	97.5	57.3%	30.9%	46.4%

Nate Jones, continued

Pitch Shape vs LHH

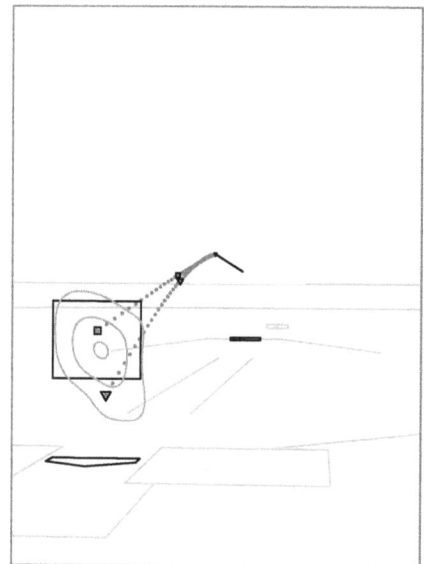

Pitch Shape vs RHH

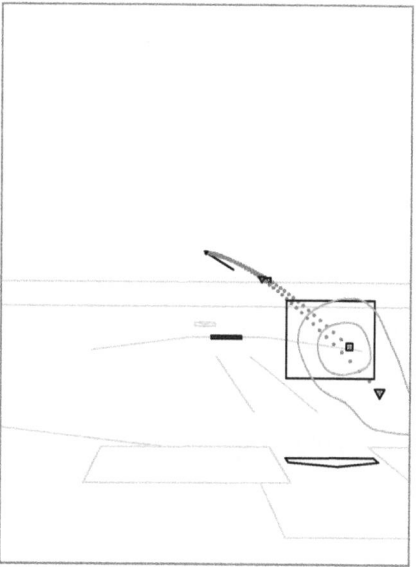

Type	Frequency	Velocity	H Movement	V Movement
☐ Sinker	51.2%	96.1 [119]	-11.4 [112]	-12.4 [126]
▽ Slider	45.8%	88.2 [119]	0.9 [83]	-27.1 [119]

Atlanta Braves 2021

Chris Martin   RHP
Born: 06/02/86   Age: 35   Bats: R   Throws: R
Height: 6'8"   Weight: 225   Origin: Round 21, 2005 Draft (#627 overall)

YEAR	TEAM	LVL	AGE	W	L	SV	G	GS	IP	H	HR	BB/9	K/9	K	GB%	BABIP
2018	TEX	MLB	32	1	5	0	46	0	41^2	46	5	1.1	8.0	37	40.9%	.323
2019	ATL	MLB	33	1	1	0	20	0	17^2	17	1	0.5	11.2	22	52.2%	.356
2019	TEX	MLB	33	0	2	4	38	0	38	35	8	0.9	10.2	43	50.0%	.293
2020	ATL	MLB	34	1	1	1	19	0	18	8	1	1.5	10.0	20	38.1%	.171
2021 FS	ATL	MLB	35	2	2	16	57	0	50	45	6	1.8	9.2	51	44.2%	.289
2021 DC	ATL	MLB	35	2	2	16	51	0	48.7	44	6	1.8	9.2	49	44.2%	.289

Comparables: Javy Guerra, Dan Otero, David Hernandez

Most people come back from vacations toting souvenirs; Martin returned stateside in 2018 with a splitter, and it's proven to be a valuable acquisition. His path to success is simple: Keep the ball down and avoid walks. Martin executed that to perfection last season, making him a valuable setup piece. Good luck sorting out his arsenal, but it's clear there's no need to fix him. (Sorry, I'm sorry, I'm trying to remove it.)

YEAR	TEAM	LVL	AGE	WHIP	ERA	DRA-	WARP	MPH	FB%	WHF	CSP
2018	TEX	MLB	32	1.22	4.54	118	-0.2	96.8	72.3%	20.4%	
2019	ATL	MLB	33	1.02	4.08	58	0.5	96.8	70.6%	28.0%	
2019	TEX	MLB	33	1.03	3.08	66	0.9	97.4	82.4%	25.5%	
2020	ATL	MLB	34	0.61	1.00	82	0.3	95.4	63.3%	26.7%	
2021 FS	ATL	MLB	35	1.11	2.99	77	0.9	96.7	73.2%	25.2%	51.5%
2021 DC	ATL	MLB	35	1.11	2.99	77	0.9	96.7	73.2%	25.2%	51.5%

Chris Martin, continued

Pitch Shape vs LHH

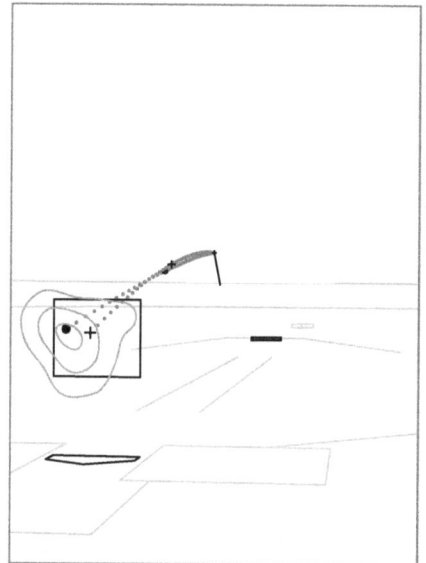

Pitch Shape vs RHH

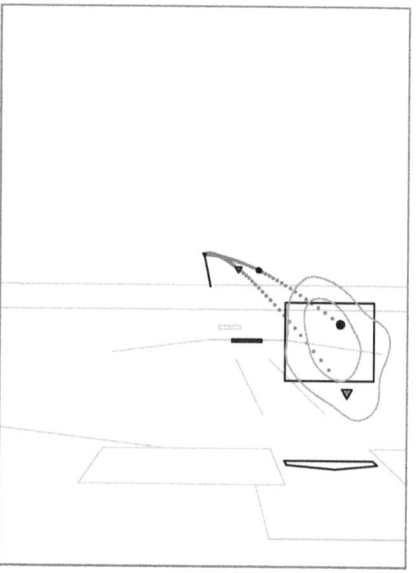

Type	Frequency	Velocity	H Movement	V Movement
● Fastball	41.8%	94.3 [105]	-7.4 [97]	-14.2 [103]
+ Cutter	18.4%	90.1 [111]	2.3 [103]	-23.3 [103]
× Splitter	10.3%	86.4 [105]	-9.4 [94]	-30.8 [95]
▽ Slider	25.9%	82.8 [95]	13 [129]	-40 [82]

Atlanta Braves 2021

Tyler Matzek LHP
Born: 10/19/90   Age: 30   Bats: L   Throws: L
Height: 6'3"   Weight: 230   Origin: Round 1, 2009 Draft (#11 overall)

YEAR	TEAM	LVL	AGE	W	L	SV	G	GS	IP	H	HR	BB/9	K/9	K	GB%	BABIP
2019	GWN	AAA	28	0	0	0	5	0	10	10	1	4.5	11.7	13	48.1%	.360
2020	ATL	MLB	29	4	3	0	21	0	29	23	1	3.1	13.3	43	45.5%	.338
2021 FS	ATL	MLB	30	2	2	4	57	0	50	42	6	5.1	11.3	62	44.5%	.303
2021 DC	ATL	MLB	30	2	2	4	45	0	48.7	41	6	5.1	11.3	61	44.5%	.303

Comparables: Kevin Gausman, Allen Webster, Erasmo Ramírez

Prior to 2020, the last time anyone had seen Matzek on a major league mound was five years ago, when he made five starts for the Rockies and walked 19 batters in 15 innings. Injuries, struggles with an anxiety disorder and a long slow bounce around the pros followed, including two separate stints with the indy league Texas AirHogs. Most busted first-round picks see their story end there, but Matzek proved such an exemplary AirHog that he landed a minor league deal with Atlanta in 2019, then completed his improbable resurrection by making the Braves' roster out of summer camp and dominating as a setup man. With newfound velocity and a slider-first approach, he's a ghost who found his way back to the land of the living, and one of the best success stories of the last decade. Kudos to him.

YEAR	TEAM	LVL	AGE	WHIP	ERA	DRA-	WARP	MPH	FB%	WHF	CSP
2019	GWN	AAA	28	1.50	9.00	79	0.2				
2020	ATL	MLB	29	1.14	2.79	59	0.9	96.4	70.8%	27.6%	
2021 FS	ATL	MLB	30	1.43	4.23	98	0.3	96.4	70.8%	27.6%	47.4%
2021 DC	ATL	MLB	30	1.43	4.23	98	0.3	96.4	70.8%	27.6%	47.4%

Tyler Matzek, continued

Pitch Shape vs LHH

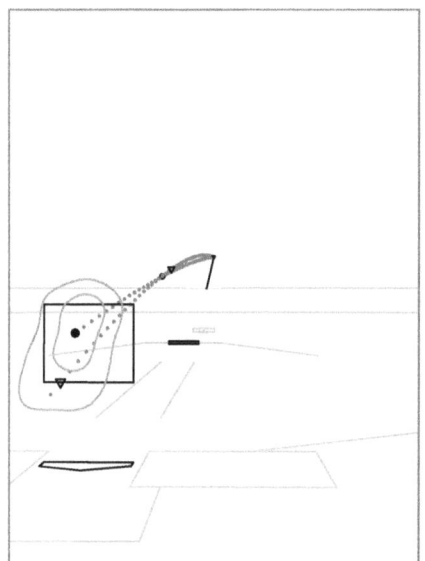

Pitch Shape vs RHH

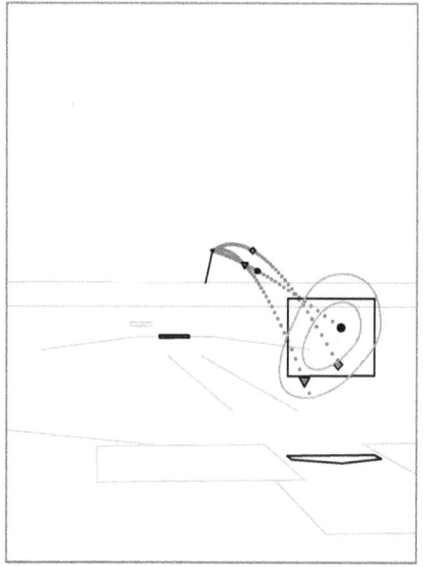

Type	Frequency	Velocity	H Movement	V Movement
● Fastball	61.8%	94.5 [106]	3.3 [116]	-11.7 [110]
+ Cutter	8.7%	90 [111]	-4.9 [120]	-24.3 [99]
▽ Slider	20.3%	83.3 [97]	-6.5 [105]	-40.9 [79]
◇ Curveball	8.7%	79.4 [103]	-8.6 [104]	-50.4 [95]

Mark Melancon RHP

Born: 03/28/85   Age: 36   Bats: R   Throws: R
Height: 6'1"   Weight: 215   Origin: Round 9, 2006 Draft (#284 overall)

YEAR	TEAM	LVL	AGE	W	L	SV	G	GS	IP	H	HR	BB/9	K/9	K	GB%	BABIP
2018	SF	MLB	33	1	4	3	41	0	39	48	2	3.2	7.2	31	50.8%	.365
2019	ATL	MLB	34	1	0	11	23	0	21	22	1	0.9	10.3	24	61.9%	.339
2019	SF	MLB	34	4	2	1	43	0	46^1	49	3	3.1	8.5	44	60.2%	.354
2020	ATL	MLB	35	2	1	11	23	0	22^2	22	1	2.8	5.6	14	58.3%	.300
2021 FS	ATL	MLB	36	2	2	13	57	0	50	49	5	2.9	7.4	40	55.8%	.294
2021 DC	ATL	MLB	36	2	2	13	47	0	41	40	4	2.9	7.4	33	55.8%	.294

Comparables: Luke Gregerson, Mariano Rivera, Will Harris

A philosophical quandary for you: Can you be a successful closer if you don't strike anyone out? Like a tree falling in an empty forest, Melancon is a conundrum. On the one hand, his strikeout rate dropped to a preposterously low 14.7 percent last season, seventh-worst in the majors among qualified relievers. On the other, he gave up a single home run all season and was scored upon in just five of 23 appearances. Melancon leans on a cutter that's far too hittable, but also throws a curveball that no one can touch. Now a free agent, general managers will pore over his seemingly contradictory stats to see if they can figure out how to get this particular goose out of the bottle. Easy, Melancon would retort: Just say, it's out.

YEAR	TEAM	LVL	AGE	WHIP	ERA	DRA-	WARP	MPH	FB%	WHF	CSP
2018	SF	MLB	33	1.59	3.23	80	0.6	92.9	68.3%	23.2%	
2019	ATL	MLB	34	1.14	3.86	44	0.7	93.4	61.2%	27.9%	
2019	SF	MLB	34	1.40	3.50	90	0.5	93.4	68.8%	24.8%	
2020	ATL	MLB	35	1.28	2.78	89	0.3	93.3	57.9%	19.6%	
2021 FS	ATL	MLB	36	1.31	3.78	90	0.5	93.3	64.5%	23.7%	45.5%
2021 DC	ATL	MLB	36	1.31	3.78	90	0.4	93.3	64.5%	23.7%	45.5%

Mark Melancon, continued

Pitch Shape vs LHH

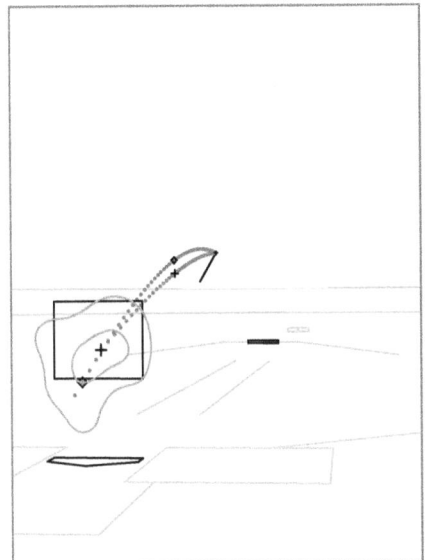

Pitch Shape vs RHH

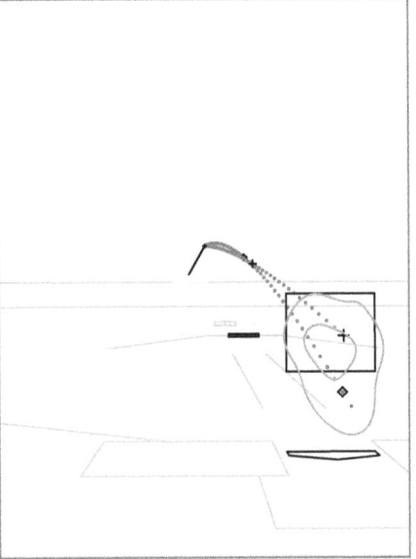

Type	Frequency	Velocity	H Movement	V Movement
+ Cutter	55.3%	92.1 [124]	1.6 [98]	-20.3 [115]
× Splitter	3.3%	84.4 [96]	-11.1 [88]	-27 [108]
◇ Curveball	37.5%	82 [113]	3.4 [83]	-50.2 [96]

Atlanta Braves 2021

Tommy Milone LHP
Born: 02/16/87 Age: 34 Bats: L Throws: L
Height: 6'0" Weight: 215 Origin: Round 10, 2008 Draft (#301 overall)

YEAR	TEAM	LVL	AGE	W	L	SV	G	GS	IP	H	HR	BB/9	K/9	K	GB%	BABIP
2018	SYR	AAA	31	7	4	0	20	20	109^2	101	11	2.0	9.3	113	35.1%	.304
2018	WAS	MLB	31	1	1	0	5	4	26^1	37	7	0.3	7.9	23	26.9%	.357
2019	TAC	AAA	32	4	2	0	9	8	49^1	49	7	2.2	7.8	43	38.3%	.286
2019	SEA	MLB	32	4	10	0	23	6	111^2	102	24	1.9	7.6	94	36.8%	.252
2020	ATL	MLB	33	1	4	0	9	9	39	55	9	1.4	9.2	40	33.8%	.374
2021 FS	ATL	MLB	34	2	2	0	57	0	50	49	8	1.8	7.9	43	36.1%	.282

Comparables: Homer Bailey, Wade Miley, Iván Nova

Spiritually a member of the Orioles for the last five years or so, Milone finally realized his destiny by joining Baltimore's patchwork rotation (and made a bid to become the internet's favorite pitcher by changing his uniform number to 69). Unfortunately, this match made in heaven was broken up by Atlanta's desperate need for starters, but Milone was unable to replicate his surprising success in Charm City with the Braves, getting torched for 16 runs in 9⅔ frames before a sore left elbow landed him on the injured list. The solution here is clear: Return Milone to where he belongs, which is throwing five mediocre innings per start as an Oriole until the sky collapses, and restore order to this particular slice of the universe.

YEAR	TEAM	LVL	AGE	WHIP	ERA	DRA-	WARP	MPH	FB%	WHF	CSP
2018	SYR	AAA	31	1.14	4.19	69	2.6				
2018	WAS	MLB	31	1.44	5.81	103	0.2	88.5	58.9%	23.3%	
2019	TAC	AAA	32	1.24	3.83	62	1.7				
2019	SEA	MLB	32	1.12	4.76	116	-0.3	88.3	43.7%	22.2%	
2020	ATL	MLB	33	1.56	6.69	122	-0.1	87.5	45.3%	27.7%	
2021 FS	ATL	MLB	34	1.19	3.81	96	0.4	88.0	45.4%	24.3%	46.0%

Tommy Milone, continued

Pitch Shape vs LHH

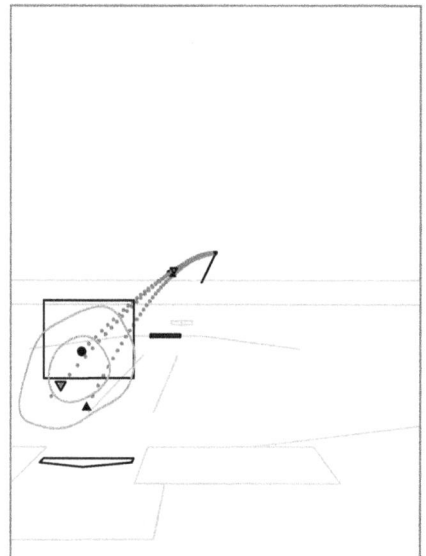

Pitch Shape vs RHH

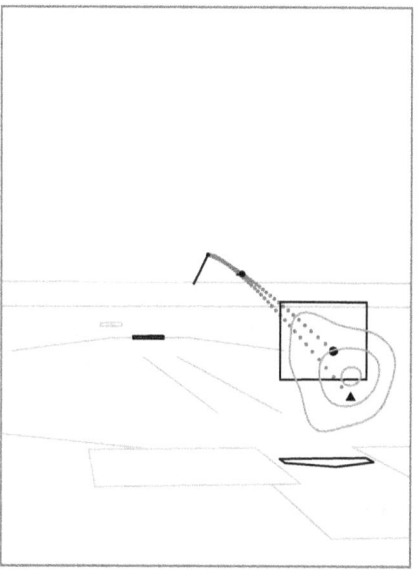

Type	Frequency	Velocity	H Movement	V Movement
● Fastball	45.2%	86.3 [80]	7.4 [97]	-16.5 [96]
▲ Changeup	39.0%	79.1 [76]	13.2 [92]	-32.1 [87]
▽ Slider	11.3%	79.7 [81]	-3.6 [94]	-33.6 [100]
◇ Curveball	4.3%	75.4 [87]	-3.1 [82]	-45.9 [106]

Atlanta Braves 2021

A.J. Minter LHP

Born: 09/02/93   Age: 27   Bats: L   Throws: L
Height: 6'0"   Weight: 215   Origin: Round 2, 2015 Draft (#75 overall)

YEAR	TEAM	LVL	AGE	W	L	SV	G	GS	IP	H	HR	BB/9	K/9	K	GB%	BABIP
2018	ATL	MLB	24	4	3	15	65	0	61^1	57	3	3.2	10.1	69	37.7%	.331
2019	GWN	AAA	25	2	2	5	20	0	22^2	24	4	1.2	11.9	30	37.7%	.351
2019	ATL	MLB	25	3	4	5	36	0	29^1	36	3	7.1	10.7	35	38.6%	.393
2020	ATL	MLB	26	1	1	0	22	0	21^2	15	1	3.7	10.0	24	48.1%	.280
2021 FS	ATL	MLB	27	2	2	4	57	0	50	42	6	3.8	10.7	59	40.4%	.292
2021 DC	ATL	MLB	27	2	2	4	45	0	48.7	41	6	3.8	10.7	58	40.4%	.292

Comparables: Aaron Bummer, Keynan Middleton, Edubray Ramos

A wild burst of, well, wildness dropped A.J. Minter from Craig Kimbrel's heir as unhittable closer in Atlanta to low-leverage project and Triple-A outcast in 2019. The lefty responded to that year from hell by pretending it never happened, quietly returning to effective setup reliever status. Buoyed by better command of his cutter and four-seamer, Minter sliced his walk rate and got more ground balls. That sets him up well to realize the role he was initially pegged for when he burst onto the scene in 2017—assuming, that is, that he doesn't flip back into the 2019 version of himself that couldn't throw a strike to save his life.

YEAR	TEAM	LVL	AGE	WHIP	ERA	DRA-	WARP	MPH	FB%	WHF	CSP
2018	ATL	MLB	24	1.29	3.23	76	1.1	98.3	49.0%	32.0%	
2019	GWN	AAA	25	1.19	3.57	55	0.8				
2019	ATL	MLB	25	2.01	7.06	122	-0.2	97.5	39.3%	30.5%	
2020	ATL	MLB	26	1.11	0.83	80	0.4	97.0	38.8%	29.1%	
2021 FS	ATL	MLB	27	1.28	3.56	86	0.6	97.6	42.0%	30.5%	46.5%
2021 DC	ATL	MLB	27	1.28	3.56	86	0.6	97.6	42.0%	30.5%	46.5%

A.J. Minter, continued

Pitch Shape vs LHH

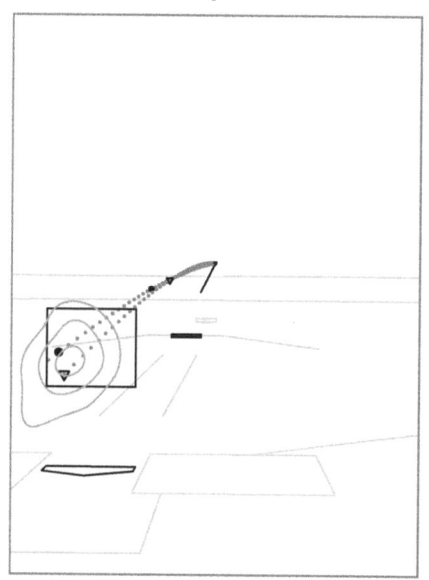

Pitch Shape vs RHH

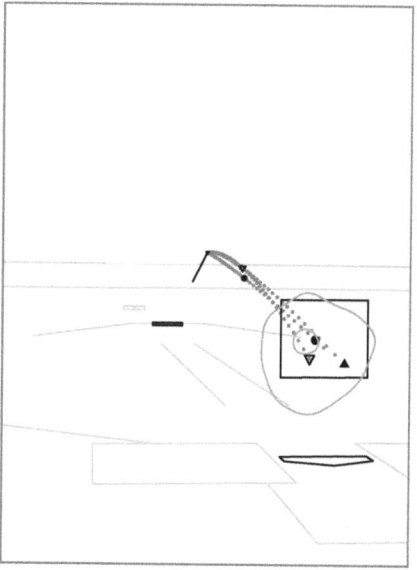

Type	Frequency	Velocity	H Movement	V Movement
● Fastball	38.0%	95.7 [110]	7.1 [98]	-11.9 [109]
▲ Changeup	18.3%	85.6 [102]	13.9 [88]	-30.9 [91]
▽ Slider	41.7%	88.1 [119]	-4 [95]	-27.8 [117]

Charlie Morton RHP

Born: 11/12/83 Age: 37 Bats: R Throws: R
Height: 6'5" Weight: 215 Origin: Round 3, 2002 Draft (#95 overall)

YEAR	TEAM	LVL	AGE	W	L	SV	G	GS	IP	H	HR	BB/9	K/9	K	GB%	BABIP
2018	HOU	MLB	34	15	3	0	30	30	167	130	18	3.4	10.8	201	47.8%	.284
2019	TB	MLB	35	16	6	0	33	33	194^2	154	15	2.6	11.1	240	47.8%	.299
2020	TB	MLB	36	2	2	0	9	9	38	43	4	2.4	9.9	42	42.1%	.355
2021 FS	ATL	MLB	37	10	7	0	26	26	150	135	17	3.1	9.8	163	46.1%	.298
2021 DC	ATL	MLB	37	9	7	0	25	25	137.3	124	16	3.1	9.8	149	46.1%	.298

Comparables: Aníbal Sánchez, Kyle Lohse, Aaron Sele

Morton had an eventful few weeks last fall. He started Game 7 of the ALCS, guiding the Rays to their second pennant in franchise history. He then had his club option declined, at which point the Rays and the Braves engaged in a bidding war for his services. The Braves won that by paying him the exact amount the Rays refused to ($15 million). As a result, it appears that he'll finish his career in Atlanta, right where it started. Morton's velocity dipped last season as he battled shoulder woes, and it's worth wondering how much he has left. That being said, few active pitchers are as intelligent or thoughtful about their craft as he is, so rest assured that he'll get the most of whatever the amount is.

YEAR	TEAM	LVL	AGE	WHIP	ERA	DRA-	WARP	MPH	FB%	WHF	CSP
2018	HOU	MLB	34	1.16	3.13	82	3.1	97.5	63.5%	28.7%	
2019	TB	MLB	35	1.08	3.05	60	5.9	96.1	50.2%	29.6%	
2020	TB	MLB	36	1.39	4.74	80	0.7	95.6	56.4%	25.0%	
2021 FS	ATL	MLB	37	1.25	3.60	88	2.4	96.3	54.6%	28.6%	50.0%
2021 DC	ATL	MLB	37	1.25	3.60	88	2.2	96.3	54.6%	28.6%	50.0%

Charlie Morton, continued

Pitch Shape vs LHH

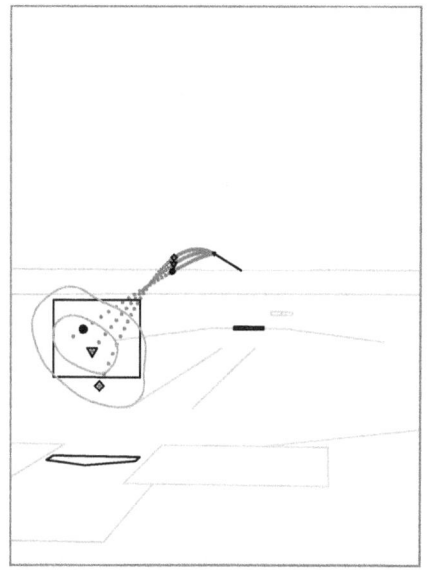

Pitch Shape vs RHH

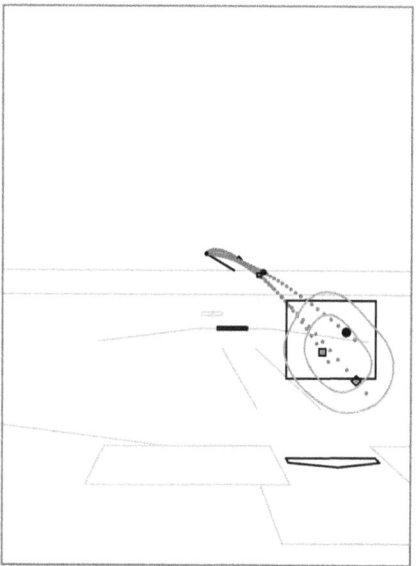

Type	Frequency	Velocity	H Movement	V Movement
● Fastball	35.6%	93.7 [104]	-9.2 [88]	-15.4 [99]
□ Sinker	20.8%	93.3 [105]	-15.8 [80]	-22.6 [93]
▽ Slider	8.8%	85.2 [106]	3.8 [95]	-31.6 [106]
◇ Curveball	32.7%	78.5 [99]	16 [134]	-48.7 [99]

Sean Newcomb LHP

Born: 06/12/93 Age: 28 Bats: L Throws: L
Height: 6'5" Weight: 255 Origin: Round 1, 2014 Draft (#15 overall)

YEAR	TEAM	LVL	AGE	W	L	SV	G	GS	IP	H	HR	BB/9	K/9	K	GB%	BABIP
2018	ATL	MLB	25	12	9	0	31	30	164	137	18	4.4	8.8	160	42.7%	.275
2019	GWN	AAA	26	2	1	0	4	3	20^2	14	1	2.2	8.7	20	45.5%	.241
2019	ATL	MLB	26	6	3	1	55	4	68^1	61	8	3.8	8.6	65	49.5%	.282
2020	ATL	MLB	27	0	2	0	4	4	13^2	20	4	4.0	6.6	10	35.3%	.340
2021 FS	ATL	MLB	28	2	2	0	57	0	50	46	6	4.7	8.9	49	43.5%	.292
2021 DC	ATL	MLB	28	3	2	0	31	3	37.3	34	5	4.7	8.9	36	43.5%	.292

Comparables: Nick Pivetta, Jordan Montgomery, Cody Reed

What does the future hold for Newcomb? A switch in 2019 from the rotation to the bullpen led to solid results; going back into the rotation this season was a full-on disaster. The biggest culprit is a fastball that was tagged for a .759 slugging percentage, offsetting all the good done by his increased usage of his changeup to go with the curveball that put him on the prospect map. None of those secondary pitches matter if your heater is getting blasted, though, and now the question becomes whether Newcomb gets one more shot as a starter or is bullpen-bound for good. His 2020 numbers don't suggest he's suited for anything other than relief.

YEAR	TEAM	LVL	AGE	WHIP	ERA	DRA-	WARP	MPH	FB%	WHF	CSP
2018	ATL	MLB	25	1.33	3.90	85	2.8	95.4	62.4%	24.9%	
2019	GWN	AAA	26	0.92	2.18	45	0.9				
2019	ATL	MLB	26	1.32	3.16	84	1.0	96.6	65.2%	22.9%	
2020	ATL	MLB	27	1.90	11.20	143	-0.2	95.0	54.0%	20.3%	
2021 FS	ATL	MLB	28	1.46	4.46	103	0.2	95.8	62.2%	23.5%	47.0%
2021 DC	ATL	MLB	28	1.46	4.46	103	0.2	95.8	62.2%	23.5%	47.0%

Sean Newcomb, continued

Pitch Shape vs LHH

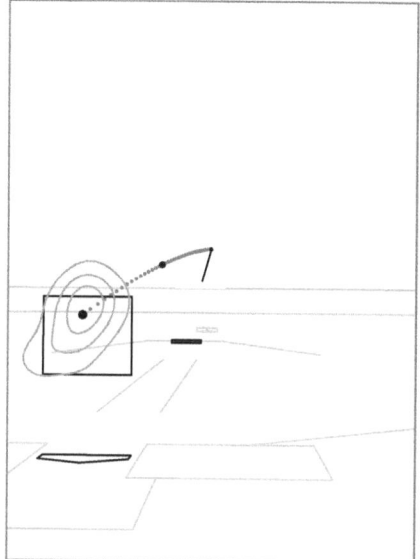

Pitch Shape vs RHH

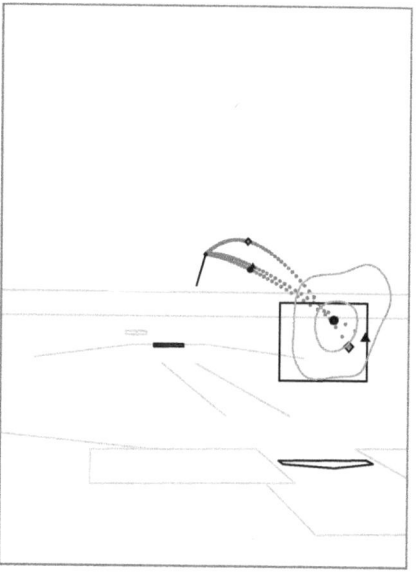

Type	Frequency	Velocity	H Movement	V Movement
● Fastball	54.0%	93.6 [103]	3.8 [114]	-13.1 [106]
▲ Changeup	20.0%	87.2 [108]	8.6 [117]	-23.6 [111]
▽ Slider	10.0%	79.8 [82]	-10.6 [120]	-47.2 [61]
◇ Curveball	16.0%	77 [94]	-8.1 [102]	-58.3 [78]

Will Smith LHP

Born: 07/10/89 Age: 31 Bats: R Throws: L
Height: 6'5" Weight: 255 Origin: Round 7, 2008 Draft (#229 overall)

YEAR	TEAM	LVL	AGE	W	L	SV	G	GS	IP	H	HR	BB/9	K/9	K	GB%	BABIP
2018	SAC	AAA	28	0	0	0	6	0	5^2	2	0	0.0	12.7	8	27.3%	.182
2018	SF	MLB	28	2	3	14	54	0	53	37	3	2.5	12.1	71	38.7%	.286
2019	SF	MLB	29	6	0	34	63	0	65^1	46	10	2.9	13.2	96	42.1%	.277
2020	ATL	MLB	30	2	2	0	18	0	16	11	7	2.2	10.1	18	30.0%	.121
2021 FS	ATL	MLB	31	3	2	16	57	0	50	40	6	3.0	11.5	63	39.1%	.288
2021 DC	ATL	MLB	31	2	2	16	51	0	48.7	39	6	3.0	11.5	62	39.1%	.288

Comparables: Jeurys Familia, Erasmo Ramírez, Trevor May

Smith probably wishes he'd stayed in the wild wild NL West for his entire career (sorry). One of the first major free agents off the board last winter, his transition from San Francisco to Atlanta didn't go off all that well; the velocity was fine, and the swings-and-misses were there. His slider wasn't, losing a lot of its sharpness and downward tilt, as opposing batters slugged a Bonds-ian .737 on that pitch despite a whiff rate of 55 percent, suggesting that both they and Smith had about the same idea of where his breaker was going once it left his hand. Add that to fewer first-pitch strikes, more fly balls and fewer swings outside the strike zone, and you can see why Smith's hard-hit rate was a not-so-jiggy 45 percent. (Again, sorry.) There's a lot in there to tweak and fix for Smith to resume being a trustworthy setup man.

YEAR	TEAM	LVL	AGE	WHIP	ERA	DRA-	WARP	MPH	FB%	WHF	CSP
2018	SAC	AAA	28	0.35	0.00	73	0.1				
2018	SF	MLB	28	0.98	2.55	74	1.0	94.3	46.1%	31.9%	
2019	SF	MLB	29	1.03	2.76	58	1.8	94.3	47.0%	34.4%	
2020	ATL	MLB	30	0.94	4.50	122	0.0	94.3	45.2%	36.7%	
2021 FS	ATL	MLB	31	1.14	2.93	75	0.9	94.3	46.4%	34.3%	46.3%
2021 DC	ATL	MLB	31	1.14	2.93	75	0.9	94.3	46.4%	34.3%	46.3%

Will Smith, continued

Pitch Shape vs LHH

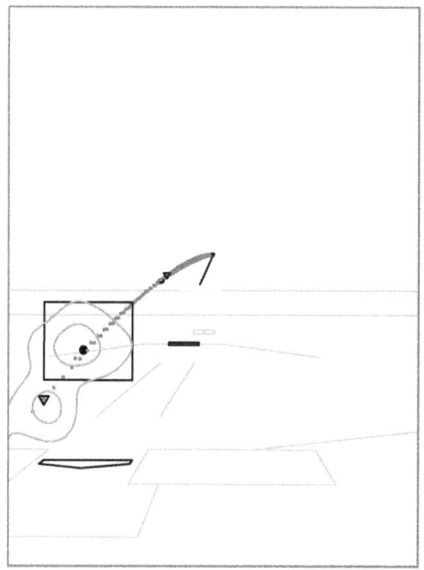

Pitch Shape vs RHH

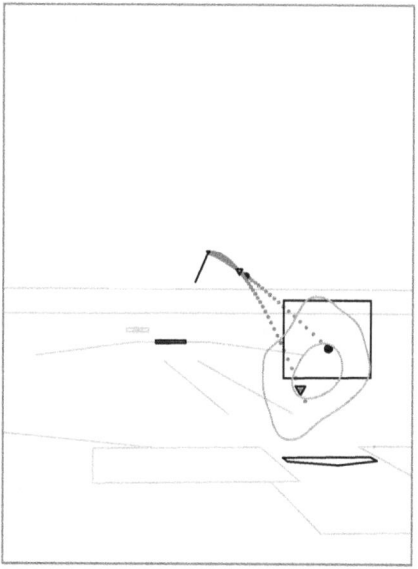

Type	Frequency	Velocity	H Movement	V Movement
● Fastball	45.2%	92.8 [101]	5.8 [104]	-14.2 [103]
▽ Slider	47.6%	81.7 [90]	-6.6 [105]	-34.8 [97]
◇ Curveball	7.1%	77.6 [96]	-8.5 [104]	-47.9 [101]

Drew Smyly LHP
Born: 06/13/89 Age: 32 Bats: L Throws: L
Height: 6'2" Weight: 188 Origin: Round 2, 2010 Draft (#68 overall)

YEAR	TEAM	LVL	AGE	W	L	SV	G	GS	IP	H	HR	BB/9	K/9	K	GB%	BABIP
2019	SA	AAA	30	1	0	0	3	3	12^2	10	2	2.1	12.8	18	27.6%	.308
2019	TEX	MLB	30	1	5	1	13	9	51^1	64	19	6.0	9.1	52	28.0%	.310
2019	PHI	MLB	30	3	2	0	12	12	62^2	62	13	3.0	9.8	68	39.3%	.310
2020	SF	MLB	31	0	1	0	7	5	26^1	20	2	3.1	14.4	42	41.7%	.310
2021 FS	ATL	MLB	32	9	8	0	26	26	150	129	24	3.5	10.9	182	35.4%	.288
2021 DC	ATL	MLB	32	4	4	0	14	14	72.7	62	11	3.5	10.9	88	35.4%	.288

Comparables: Tyler Thornburg, Anthony Bass, Alex Colomé

There's a narrative beat in many superhero films when the protagonist who discovers superpowers shortly thereafter finds out about a weakness, limit or downside to those powers: Superman, meet Kryptonite. Avengers, sorry about that Thanos snap. Between the moment of discovery and the reassertion of vulnerability exists a giddy state of euphoria: Could this be real? Is it me doing these things? We shouldn't blame the injury-plagued Smyly if he feels that way after rediscovering a fastball that tickles the mid-90s, which he mainly paired with his looping, 80 mph curve to devastating effect. For his brief time on the mound in 2020, this late-career velocity surge helped turn him into a dominant whiff-machine. It's all-too easy to see the foreshadowing of the coming *hamartia* in Smyly's checkered injury past, or in his difficulty navigating through an opposing lineup a third time. His recent powers, however, should be enough to merit the free agent a look by any team whose rotation is more *Galaxy Quest* than *Justice League*.

YEAR	TEAM	LVL	AGE	WHIP	ERA	DRA-	WARP	MPH	FB%	WHF	CSP
2019	SA	AAA	30	1.03	4.97	51	0.5				
2019	TEX	MLB	30	1.91	8.42	198	-2.2	92.5	52.8%	23.9%	
2019	PHI	MLB	30	1.32	4.45	104	0.4	93.3	43.1%	27.9%	
2020	SF	MLB	31	1.10	3.42	64	0.7	95.4	45.6%	34.7%	
2021 FS	ATL	MLB	32	1.26	3.69	90	2.3	93.6	47.4%	28.2%	47.4%
2021 DC	ATL	MLB	32	1.26	3.69	90	1.1	93.6	47.4%	28.2%	47.4%

Drew Smyly, continued

Pitch Shape vs LHH

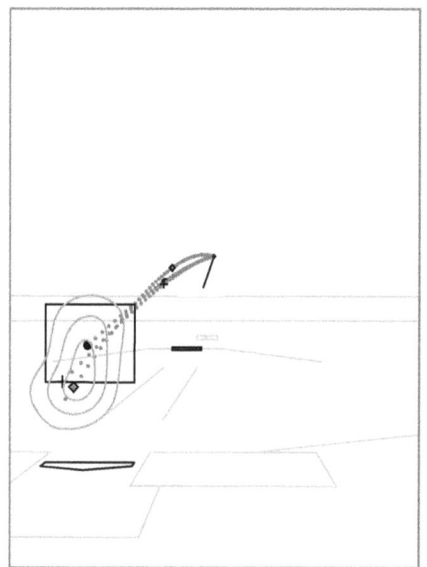

Pitch Shape vs RHH

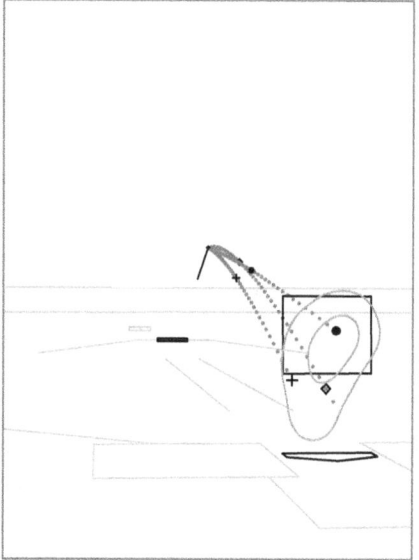

Type	Frequency	Velocity	H Movement	V Movement
● Fastball	45.6%	93.7 [104]	5.2 [107]	-11.6 [110]
+ Cutter	18.1%	89.3 [106]	-0.4 [90]	-21.2 [112]
◇ Curveball	36.3%	79.9 [105]	3.2 [56]	-41.2 [116]

Mike Soroka   RHP

Born: 08/04/97   Age: 23   Bats: R   Throws: R
Height: 6'5"   Weight: 225   Origin: Round 1, 2015 Draft (#28 overall)

YEAR	TEAM	LVL	AGE	W	L	SV	G	GS	IP	H	HR	BB/9	K/9	K	GB%	BABIP
2018	GWN	AAA	20	2	1	0	5	5	27	20	0	2.0	10.3	31	70.1%	.299
2018	ATL	MLB	20	2	1	0	5	5	25²	30	1	2.5	7.4	21	43.5%	.349
2019	GWN	AAA	21	1	0	0	2	2	9¹	5	1	1.0	9.6	10	72.7%	.190
2019	ATL	MLB	21	13	4	0	29	29	174²	153	14	2.1	7.3	142	50.6%	.282
2020	ATL	MLB	22	0	1	0	3	3	13²	11	0	4.6	5.3	8	61.0%	.268
2021 FS	ATL	MLB	23	9	8	0	26	26	150	149	18	2.8	7.7	127	51.5%	.296
2021 DC	ATL	MLB	23	10	8	0	27	27	156.7	156	18	2.8	7.7	133	51.5%	.296

Comparables: Brett Anderson, Madison Bumgarner, Roger Clemens

Soroka, we hardly knew ya: The breakout star of Atlanta's 2019 campaign made it all of three starts into 2020 before he tore his right Achilles tendon in early August, knocking him out for the rest of the year. It's not worth reading into his results too much, given how puny a sample size we're talking about; more important is that his stuff looked much the same as they did the year prior (though his fastball remains alarmingly straight). Assuming a full recovery from surgery, the baby-faced Canadian will resume his place atop the Braves' rotation alongside fellow tots Anderson and Fried. Still just 23, his future remains incandescent so long as he avoids further injury.

YEAR	TEAM	LVL	AGE	WHIP	ERA	DRA-	WARP	MPH	FB%	WHF	CSP
2018	GWN	AAA	20	0.96	2.00	59	0.8				
2018	ATL	MLB	20	1.44	3.51	103	0.2	94.4	68.9%	22.2%	
2019	GWN	AAA	21	0.64	3.86	45	0.4				
2019	ATL	MLB	21	1.11	2.68	66	4.8	94.5	63.3%	22.7%	
2020	ATL	MLB	22	1.32	3.95	94	0.2	94.3	59.3%	22.6%	
2021 FS	ATL	MLB	23	1.31	3.90	94	1.9	94.5	63.3%	22.7%	47.7%
2021 DC	ATL	MLB	23	1.31	3.90	94	2.0	94.5	63.3%	22.7%	47.7%

Mike Soroka, continued

Pitch Shape vs LHH

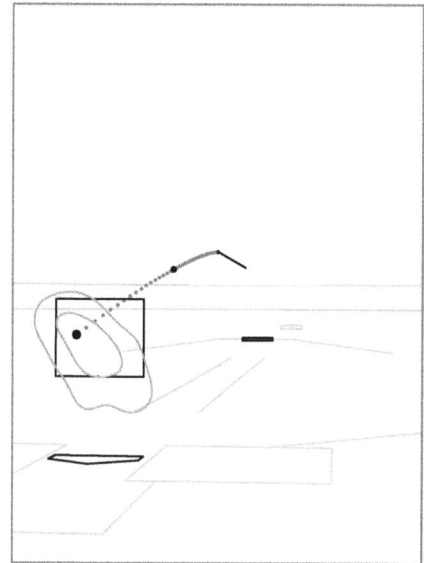

Pitch Shape vs RHH

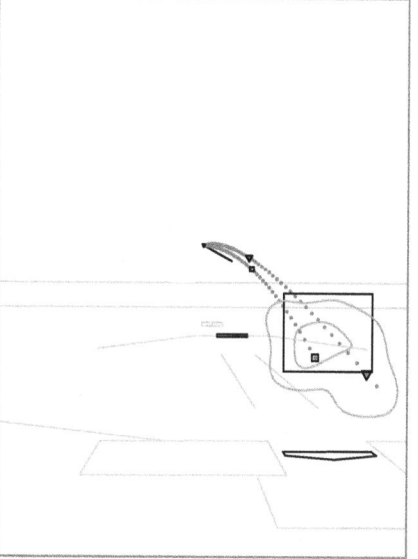

Type	Frequency	Velocity	H Movement	V Movement
● Fastball	28.1%	93 [101]	-5.9 [104]	-16.7 [96]
☐ Sinker	31.2%	91.7 [96]	-13.7 [95]	-23.2 [91]
▲ Changeup	12.1%	80.5 [82]	-13.6 [90]	-27.8 [99]
▽ Slider	28.6%	81.5 [89]	4.8 [98]	-39.9 [82]

Braves Player Analysis - 73

Josh Tomlin RHP

Born: 10/19/84 Age: 36 Bats: R Throws: R
Height: 6'1" Weight: 190 Origin: Round 19, 2006 Draft (#581 overall)

YEAR	TEAM	LVL	AGE	W	L	SV	G	GS	IP	H	HR	BB/9	K/9	K	GB%	BABIP
2018	COL	AAA	33	0	1	0	3	3	9^1	19	3	0.0	7.7	8	34.2%	.457
2018	CLE	MLB	33	2	5	0	32	9	70^1	92	25	1.5	5.9	46	31.7%	.286
2019	ATL	MLB	34	2	1	2	51	1	79^1	82	14	0.8	5.8	51	33.2%	.279
2020	ATL	MLB	35	2	2	0	17	5	39^2	40	6	1.8	8.2	36	38.1%	.306
2021 FS	ATL	MLB	36	2	2	0	57	0	50	52	9	1.5	7.0	39	36.5%	.285
2021 DC	ATL	MLB	36	6	3	0	43	3	55.3	58	11	1.5	7.0	43	36.5%	.285

Comparables: Ian Kennedy, Jason Vargas, Jason Hammel

That Tomlin finished second on the Braves in innings pitched in 2020 is as easy a way as any to show how utterly pear-shaped things got for them, pitching-wise. That he was one of their more reliable arms gets the point across too. The veteran righty wasn't able to keep up the entirety of the late-career resurgence that was his 2019 in Atlanta, though the fact that he's still contributing at age 35 and with a fastball that putters in at 88 mph is something of a miracle on its own. Perhaps aware that you can't live life in the slow lane, Tomlin threw more cutters and curveballs into the mix, but his gains—a big spike in strikeout rate—were offset by poor results on those pitches anyway, particularly the curve. There's value in what he offers, which is to say gobbling up innings like Mr. Creosote, but league-average work is the best you can hope for.

YEAR	TEAM	LVL	AGE	WHIP	ERA	DRA-	WARP	MPH	FB%	WHF	CSP
2018	COL	AAA	33	2.04	6.75	102	0.1				
2018	CLE	MLB	33	1.48	6.14	153	-1.4	89.5	72.5%	19.3%	
2019	ATL	MLB	34	1.12	3.74	108	0.1	90.5	74.0%	19.9%	
2020	ATL	MLB	35	1.21	4.76	94	0.5	89.3	70.1%	22.9%	
2021 FS	ATL	MLB	36	1.22	4.20	104	0.1	89.9	72.4%	20.8%	48.5%
2021 DC	ATL	MLB	36	1.22	4.20	104	0.2	89.9	72.4%	20.8%	48.5%

Josh Tomlin, continued

Pitch Shape vs LHH

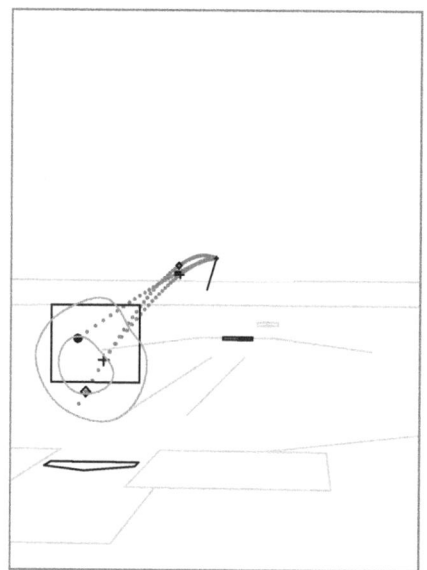

Pitch Shape vs RHH

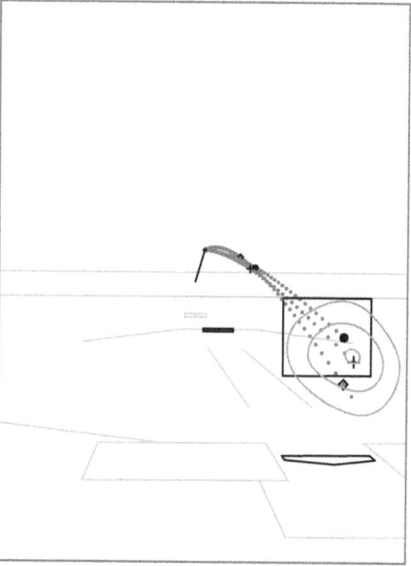

Type	Frequency	Velocity	H Movement	V Movement
● Fastball	19.0%	88.4 [87]	-7.9 [94]	-16 [98]
+ Cutter	50.1%	85.8 [84]	2.2 [102]	-23.7 [102]
▲ Changeup	3.8%	84.1 [96]	-12.4 [96]	-26.7 [102]
◇ Curveball	25.7%	76.6 [92]	3.8 [85]	-46.9 [103]

Braves Player Analysis - 75

Touki Toussaint RHP
Born: 06/20/96 Age: 25 Bats: R Throws: R
Height: 6'3" Weight: 215 Origin: Round 1, 2014 Draft (#16 overall)

YEAR	TEAM	LVL	AGE	W	L	SV	G	GS	IP	H	HR	BB/9	K/9	K.	GB%	BABIP
2018	MIS	AA	22	4	6	0	16	16	86	66	7	3.8	11.2	107	46.5%	.286
2018	GWN	AAA	22	5	0	0	8	8	50^1	35	0	3.0	10.0	56	43.2%	.280
2018	ATL	MLB	22	2	1	0	7	5	29	18	1	6.5	9.9	32	45.6%	.258
2019	GWN	AAA	23	1	6	0	10	10	39^2	51	5	6.4	10.0	44	41.8%	.393
2019	ATL	MLB	23	4	0	0	24	1	41^2	44	5	5.6	9.7	45	42.5%	.345
2020	ATL	MLB	24	0	2	0	7	5	24^1	27	7	5.9	11.1	30	37.7%	.328
2021 FS	ATL	MLB	25	2	3	0	57	0	50	46	7	5.6	9.8	54	41.5%	.299
2021 DC	ATL	MLB	25	3	2	0	26	3	38	35	5	5.6	9.8	41	41.5%	.299

Comparables: Sean Reid-Foley, Zack Littell, Robert Stephenson

Toussaint's 2020 was so ghastly and depressing that it should qualify for pandemic assistance. Putting up the equivalent of Dylan Cease's year but without any of Cease's luck, Toussaint made it past the fourth inning in exactly one of his five starts, while the slider he started throwing in place of his non-competitive sinker was hit so hard that he basically abandoned it by season's end. On the plus side, his four-seamer still sits at 94 mph (albeit with below-average spin and movement), and his curveball and splitter are true weapons. The talent is still there. It just looks more and more like said talent will be making a home for itself in the bullpen.

YEAR	TEAM	LVL	AGE	WHIP	ERA	DRA-	WARP	MPH	FB%	WHF	CSP
2018	MIS	AA	22	1.19	2.93	84	1.4				
2018	GWN	AAA	22	1.03	1.43	73	1.1				
2018	ATL	MLB	22	1.34	4.03	104	0.2	95.7	53.4%	27.4%	
2019	GWN	AAA	23	1.99	7.49	140	0.0				
2019	ATL	MLB	23	1.68	5.62	98	0.3	95.6	49.2%	29.8%	
2020	ATL	MLB	24	1.77	8.88	113	0.1	96.3	41.1%	31.9%	
2021 FS	ATL	MLB	25	1.56	5.12	112	-0.1	95.9	46.4%	30.3%	42.0%
2021 DC	ATL	MLB	25	1.56	5.12	112	0.0	95.9	46.4%	30.3%	42.0%

Touki Toussaint, continued

Pitch Shape vs LHH

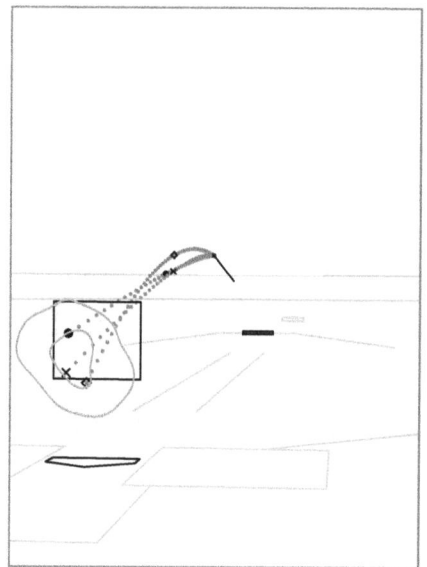

Pitch Shape vs RHH

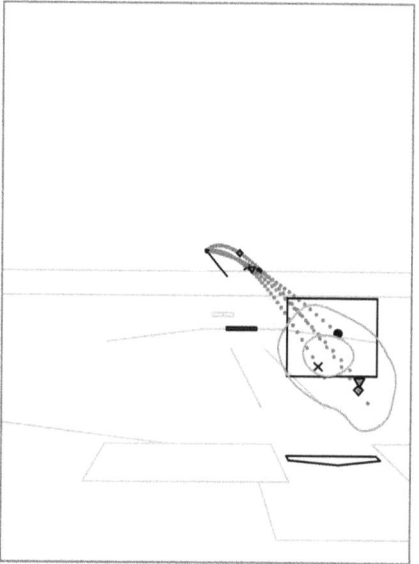

Type	Frequency	Velocity	H Movement	V Movement
● Fastball	36.0%	94.3 [105]	-6.8 [99]	-15 [100]
□ Sinker	5.1%	92.8 [102]	-15 [85]	-23.6 [90]
✕ Splitter	20.4%	85.5 [101]	-7.9 [100]	-31.7 [92]
▽ Slider	9.6%	85.7 [108]	4.3 [97]	-33.3 [101]
◇ Curveball	28.8%	76 [90]	11.6 [117]	-55.5 [84]

Atlanta Braves 2021

Jacob Webb RHP
Born: 08/15/93   Age: 27   Bats: R   Throws: R
Height: 6'2"   Weight: 210   Origin: Round 18, 2014 Draft (#553 overall)

YEAR	TEAM	LVL	AGE	W	L	SV	G	GS	IP	H	HR	BB/9	K/9	K	GB%	BABIP
2018	MIS	AA	24	1	2	7	21	0	22²	16	4	4.8	13.9	35	39.2%	.273
2018	GWN	AAA	24	2	2	11	30	0	31²	20	3	3.1	9.7	34	40.7%	.218
2019	GWN	AAA	25	0	1	1	10	0	10¹	9	1	7.8	10.5	12	50.0%	.296
2019	ATL	MLB	25	4	0	2	36	0	32¹	24	4	3.3	7.8	28	38.9%	.235
2020	ATL	MLB	26	0	0	0	8	0	10	7	0	4.5	9.0	10	60.0%	.280
2021 FS	ATL	MLB	27	2	2	0	57	0	50	42	6	4.1	9.8	54	42.5%	.279
2021 DC	ATL	MLB	27	2	2	0	45	0	48.7	41	6	4.1	9.8	53	42.5%	.279

Comparables: Sam Tuivailala, Edubray Ramos, Jensen Lewis

There's something to be said about being the guy your team turns to when nothing matters anymore. That was Webb, whose eight September appearances had an average leverage index of .08—the statistical definition of "no pressure, kid."

YEAR	TEAM	LVL	AGE	WHIP	ERA	DRA-	WARP	MPH	FB%	WHF	CSP
2018	MIS	AA	24	1.24	3.18	58	0.6				
2018	GWN	AAA	24	0.98	3.13	62	0.7				
2019	GWN	AAA	25	1.74	6.97	91	0.2				
2019	ATL	MLB	25	1.11	1.39	100	0.2	96.3	54.5%	26.2%	
2020	ATL	MLB	26	1.20	0.00	85	0.2	94.5	52.4%	32.9%	
2021 FS	ATL	MLB	27	1.31	3.68	88	0.6	95.7	53.8%	28.4%	46.6%
2021 DC	ATL	MLB	27	1.31	3.68	88	0.6	95.7	53.8%	28.4%	46.6%

Jacob Webb, continued

Pitch Shape vs LHH

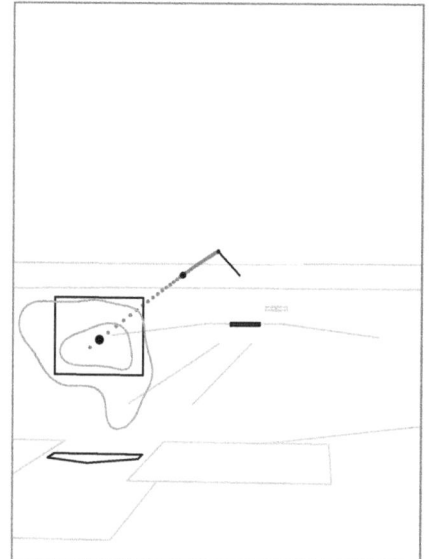

Pitch Shape vs RHH

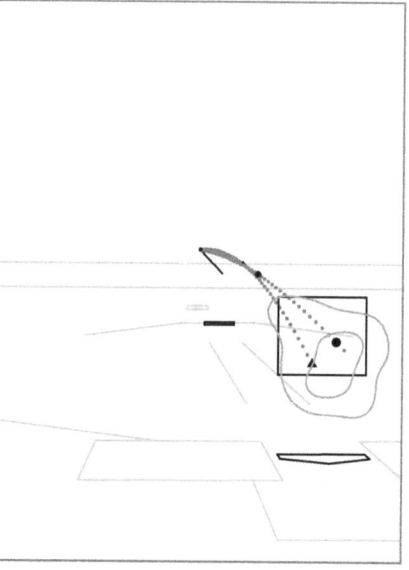

Type	Frequency	Velocity	H Movement	V Movement
● Fastball	51.5%	93.7 [104]	-12.4 [73]	-13.7 [104]
▲ Changeup	32.2%	82.5 [90]	-15.8 [78]	-29.6 [94]
◇ Curveball	14.6%	80.4 [107]	4.1 [86]	-44.3 [109]

Atlanta Braves 2021

Bryse Wilson RHP
Born: 12/20/97 Age: 23 Bats: R Throws: R
Height: 6'2" Weight: 225 Origin: Round 4, 2016 Draft (#109 overall)

YEAR	TEAM	LVL	AGE	W	L	SV	G	GS	IP	H	HR	BB/9	K/9	K	GB%	BABIP
2018	FLO	HI-A	20	2	0	0	5	5	26²	16	0	2.4	8.8	26	57.1%	.229
2018	MIS	AA	20	3	5	0	15	15	77	77	3	3.0	10.4	89	41.7%	.354
2018	GWN	AAA	20	3	0	0	5	3	22	20	6	1.2	11.5	28	42.9%	.280
2018	ATL	MLB	20	1	0	0	3	1	7	8	0	7.7	7.7	6	28.6%	.381
2019	GWN	AAA	21	10	7	0	21	21	121	120	12	1.9	8.8	118	44.7%	.315
2019	ATL	MLB	21	1	1	0	6	4	20	26	5	4.5	7.2	16	31.3%	.350
2020	ATL	MLB	22	1	0	1	6	2	15²	18	2	5.2	8.6	15	43.8%	.348
2021 FS	ATL	MLB	23	2	2	0	57	0	50	48	8	3.2	8.2	45	41.0%	.285
2021 DC	ATL	MLB	23	4	3	0	37	3	40	39	7	3.2	8.2	36	41.0%	.285

Comparables: Lucas Giolito, Jaime Barria, David Holmberg

Like the rest of us, Wilson clearly spent his quarantine trying to learn how to bake, and like the rest of us, the results were mixed. The fastball that is his bread and butter didn't spend enough time proofing, with opposing batters slugging .607 against it. His attempts to refine his slider went over about as well as your attempt to make a sourdough starter. His control—summarized by a walk rate of 12.3 percent—needed more time in the oven. But despite all those issues, Wilson soldiered through a solid-enough season split between the rotation and bullpen and capped it all off with a stellar start against the Dodgers in the NLCS, holding the eventual champs to one run over six innings. That'll earn him a Paul Hollywood handshake and likely a chance to win a spot in the back of the rotation, if Atlanta doesn't fill that hole this winter.

YEAR	TEAM	LVL	AGE	WHIP	ERA	DRA-	WARP	MPH	FB%	WHF	CSP
2018	FLO	HI-A	20	0.86	0.34	80	0.5				
2018	MIS	AA	20	1.34	3.97	83	1.3				
2018	GWN	AAA	20	1.05	5.32	68	0.5				
2018	ATL	MLB	20	2.00	6.43	120	0.0	96.4	71.1%	30.4%	
2019	GWN	AAA	21	1.21	3.42	67	4.0				
2019	ATL	MLB	21	1.80	7.20	149	-0.3	96.7	72.8%	20.5%	
2020	ATL	MLB	22	1.72	4.02	105	0.1	95.7	81.8%	21.2%	
2021 FS	ATL	MLB	23	1.34	4.38	103	0.1	96.1	77.4%	21.6%	47.1%
2021 DC	ATL	MLB	23	1.34	4.38	103	0.2	96.1	77.4%	21.6%	47.1%

Bryse Wilson, continued

Pitch Shape vs LHH

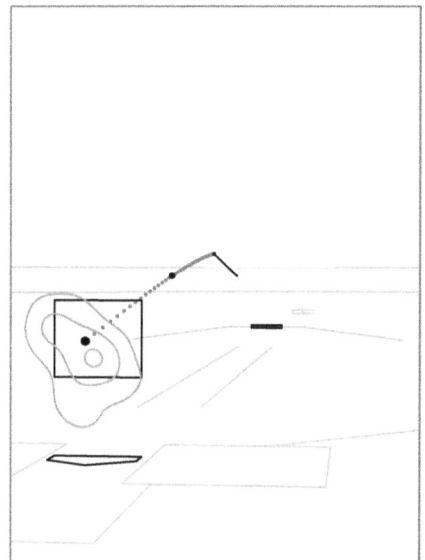

Pitch Shape vs RHH

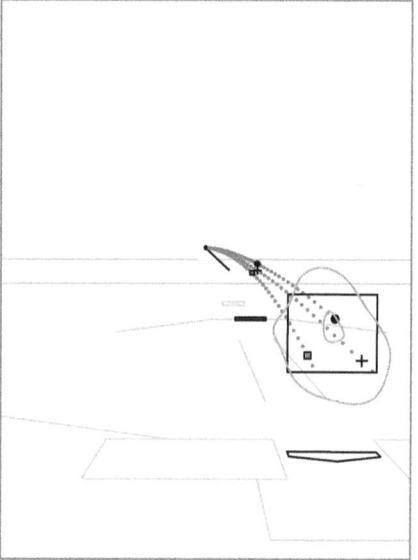

Type	Frequency	Velocity	H Movement	V Movement
● Fastball	46.0%	94.3 [106]	-7.2 [97]	-14.6 [102]
☐ Sinker	16.9%	93.3 [105]	-14.9 [87]	-21.6 [97]
+ Cutter	18.8%	88.8 [103]	1.6 [98]	-23.6 [102]
▲ Changeup	11.5%	87.1 [108]	-11.7 [100]	-27.1 [101]
◇ Curveball	6.7%	78.9 [101]	14.8 [129]	-37.5 [124]

Atlanta Braves 2021

Kyle Wright RHP
Born: 10/02/95 Age: 25 Bats: R Throws: R
Height: 6'4" Weight: 215 Origin: Round 1, 2017 Draft (#5 overall)

YEAR	TEAM	LVL	AGE	W	L	SV	G	GS	IP	H	HR	BB/9	K/9	K	GB%	BABIP
2018	MIS	AA	22	6	8	0	20	20	109^1	103	6	3.5	8.6	105	53.1%	.317
2018	GWN	AAA	22	2	1	0	7	4	28^2	15	2	2.5	8.8	28	49.3%	.186
2018	ATL	MLB	22	0	0	0	4	0	6	4	2	9.0	7.5	5	41.2%	.133
2019	GWN	AAA	23	11	4	0	21	21	112^1	107	13	2.8	9.3	116	47.3%	.314
2019	ATL	MLB	23	0	3	0	7	4	19^2	24	4	5.9	8.2	18	41.0%	.351
2020	ATL	MLB	24	2	4	0	8	8	38	35	7	5.7	7.1	30	44.7%	.262
2021 FS	ATL	MLB	25	9	8	0	26	26	150	142	20	4.3	8.2	136	45.8%	.287
2021 DC	ATL	MLB	25	2	2	0	9	8	38	36	5	4.3	8.2	34	45.8%	.287

Comparables: Reynaldo López, Mitch Keller, Zack Littell

Remember sitting in math class in high school, looking around as your friends breezed through trigonometry and calculus problem, and then wondering why your own homework was such a mess? That was Wright, glumly trying to remember the quadratic formula as his fellow former first-round rotation-mates all mastered sine curves and tangents. It's an especially confounding state of affairs given that Wright throws 95 mph with an easy, simple delivery. The problem is that 95 doesn't mean much if your fastball has no action behind it, and his heater is as bland and hittable as they come. Understandably, Wright swapped his four-seamer for his sinker, which proved harder to square up, but his strikeout rate remained anemic, and there's not much daylight between it and his walk rate. Given that his postseason offered no real clues to his future, better control and adjustments to the fastball are paramount to Wright passing this particular class.

YEAR	TEAM	LVL	AGE	WHIP	ERA	DRA-	WARP	MPH	FB%	WHF	CSP
2018	MIS	AA	22	1.34	3.70	82	1.9				
2018	GWN	AAA	22	0.80	2.51	82	0.5				
2018	ATL	MLB	22	1.67	4.50	111	0.0	95.3	51.6%	28.9%	
2019	GWN	AAA	23	1.26	4.17	72	3.4				
2019	ATL	MLB	23	1.88	8.69	129	-0.1	96.5	54.4%	23.8%	
2020	ATL	MLB	24	1.55	5.21	124	-0.2	96.3	48.4%	24.0%	
2021 FS	ATL	MLB	25	1.43	4.46	103	1.2	96.3	50.1%	24.2%	43.2%
2021 DC	ATL	MLB	25	1.43	4.46	103	0.3	96.3	50.1%	24.2%	43.2%

Kyle Wright, continued

Pitch Shape vs LHH	Pitch Shape vs RHH
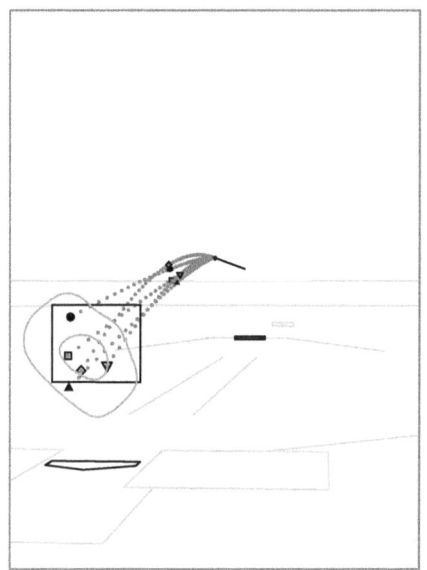	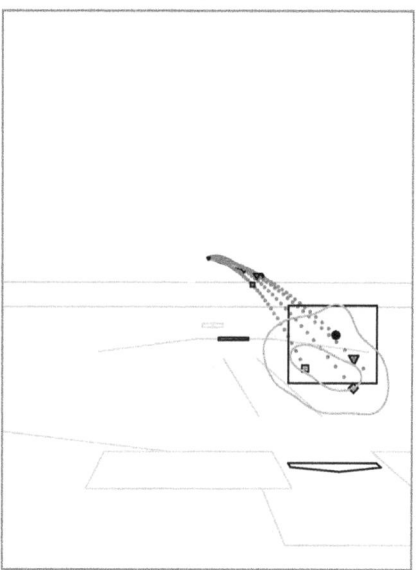

Type	Frequency	Velocity	H Movement	V Movement
● Fastball	15.7%	95.1 [108]	-9.6 [86]	-14.9 [101]
□ Sinker	32.6%	94.2 [109]	-14.1 [92]	-20.1 [101]
▲ Changeup	14.3%	87.9 [111]	-13.9 [89]	-26 [104]
▽ Slider	24.1%	88.5 [120]	2 [88]	-26.4 [121]
◇ Curveball	13.1%	82.3 [114]	12 [118]	-41.7 [115]

Huascar Ynoa RHP

Born: 05/28/98 Age: 23 Bats: R Throws: R
Height: 6'2" Weight: 220 Origin: International Free Agent, 2014

YEAR	TEAM	LVL	AGE	W	L	SV	G	GS	IP	H	HR	BB/9	K/9	K	GB%	BABIP
2018	ROM	LO-A	20	7	8	0	18	18	91^2	69	7	4.1	9.8	100	46.3%	.264
2018	FLO	HI-A	20	1	4	0	6	6	24^2	33	1	4.4	11.3	31	44.6%	.444
2019	FLO	HI-A	21	0	1	0	3	3	11	10	0	4.9	13.1	16	59.3%	.370
2019	MIS	AA	21	1	2	1	6	0	13^2	17	2	3.3	9.9	15	65.1%	.375
2019	GWN	AAA	21	3	5	0	17	14	72^2	80	14	4.2	9.8	79	42.7%	.332
2019	ATL	MLB	21	0	0	0	2	0	3	6	1	3.0	9.0	3	41.7%	.455
2020	ATL	MLB	22	0	0	0	9	5	21^2	23	2	5.4	7.1	17	55.9%	.318
2021 FS	ATL	MLB	23	2	3	0	57	0	50	48	6	5.0	8.3	46	47.6%	.293
2021 DC	ATL	MLB	23	4	3	0	37	3	43.3	41	5	5.0	8.3	40	47.6%	.293

Comparables: Luis Severino, Pedro Avila, Rony García

One of the many young arms pressed into service by Atlanta's rash of pitching injuries, Ynoa didn't make the most of his opportunity in the rotation. To be fair, the Braves used him more as an opener than a traditional starter, but you have to squint to find much good in those outings. Like Toussaint, Wilson and Wright, Ynoa needs to work on his control and do something about a fastball that sits at 95 mph but elicits no swings and misses. His slider produced better returns, but there's no consistent third pitch, as he threw his changeup just 33 times all season. Everything about Ynoa's profile screams "middle reliever, and not a particularly good one," and the Braves have so many of those arms that he's going to have a tough time emerging from a crowded group.

YEAR	TEAM	LVL	AGE	WHIP	ERA	DRA-	WARP	MPH	FB%	WHF	CSP
2018	ROM	LO-A	20	1.21	3.63	84	1.3				
2018	FLO	HI-A	20	1.82	8.03	80	0.4				
2019	FLO	HI-A	21	1.45	3.27	80	0.2				
2019	MIS	AA	21	1.61	5.27	112	-0.1				
2019	GWN	AAA	21	1.57	5.33	104	1.1				
2019	ATL	MLB	21	2.33	18.00	137	0.0	98.8	60.6%	24.1%	
2020	ATL	MLB	22	1.66	5.82	90	0.3	97.4	44.3%	25.5%	
2021 FS	ATL	MLB	23	1.52	4.81	108	0.0	97.5	45.9%	25.4%	45.2%
2021 DC	ATL	MLB	23	1.52	4.81	108	0.1	97.5	45.9%	25.4%	45.2%

Huascar Ynoa, continued

Pitch Shape vs LHH
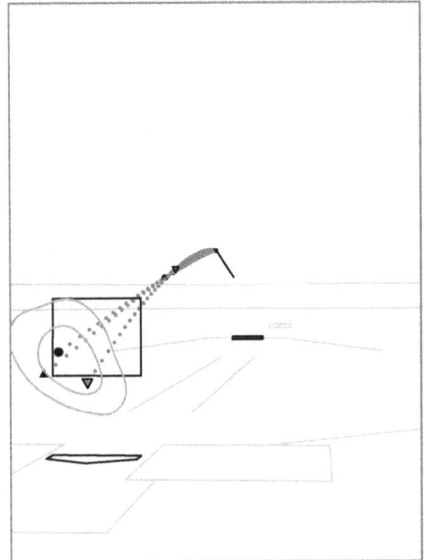

Pitch Shape vs RHH
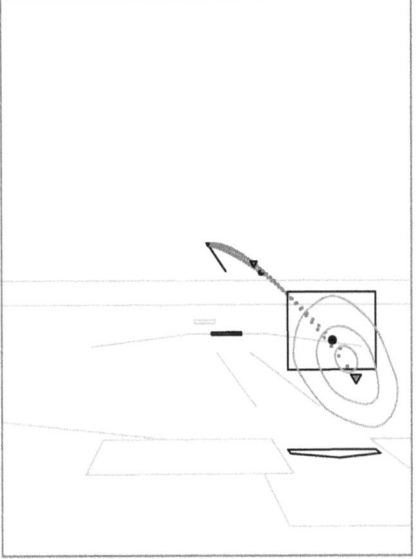

Type	Frequency	Velocity	H Movement	V Movement
● Fastball	44.0%	95 [108]	-8.4 [92]	-13.4 [105]
▲ Changeup	9.0%	86.8 [106]	-13.1 [93]	-23.1 [112]
▽ Slider	46.2%	86.2 [110]	0.9 [84]	-34.4 [98]

PLAYER COMMENTS WITHOUT GRAPHS

Abraham Almonte RF
Born: 06/27/89   Age: 32   Bats: S   Throws: R
Height: 5'10"   Weight: 223   Origin: International Free Agent, 2005

YEAR	TEAM	LVL	AGE	PA	R	2B	3B	HR	RBI	BB	K	SB	CS	AVG/OBP/SLG
2018	KC	MLB	29	151	15	1	2	3	9	15	36	2	2	.179/.260/.284
2019	RNO	AAA	30	382	78	33	4	17	59	60	70	12	3	.270/.382/.558
2019	ARI	MLB	30	38	11	3	1	1	4	7	8	0	0	.290/.421/.548
2020	SD	MLB	31	13	0	0	0	0	0	2	4	1	1	.091/.231/.091
2021 FS	ATL	MLB	32	600	67	21	4	15	60	64	152	8	3	.209/.296/.353
2021 DC	ATL	MLB	32	198	22	7	1	4	19	21	50	2	1	.209/.296/.353

Comparables: Cameron Maybin, Pete Whisenant, Corey Patterson

The Padres decided to bring back Almonte for a second stint, perhaps with the hope that his hot September the previous year was an indication of improved plate discipline and power. It wasn't; though, to be fair, the Padres barely gave him a chance to do much of anything. Almonte signed with the Braves before Halloween, suggesting he's comfortable with prioritizing a ring over swings.

YEAR	TEAM	LVL	AGE	PA	DRC+	BABIP	BRR	FRAA	WARP
2018	KC	MLB	29	151	68	.219	1.1	CF(35): 0.2, RF(3): 0.0, LF(1): -0.1	0.0
2019	RNO	AAA	30	382	119	.294	0.5	CF(58): -2.9, RF(31): -1.6, LF(4): 1.2	1.8
2019	ARI	MLB	30	38	93	.364	2.1	RF(9): 0.2, CF(3): -0.2	0.3
2020	SD	MLB	31	13	92	.143	-0.4	LF(2): 0.3, CF(1): -0.0	0.0
2021 FS	ATL	MLB	32	600	81	.262	0.7	RF 0, LF 4	0.7
2021 DC	ATL	MLB	32	198	81	.262	0.2	RF 0, LF 1	0.1

William Contreras C

Born: 12/24/97 Age: 23 Bats: R Throws: R
Height: 6'0" Weight: 180 Origin: International Free Agent, 2015

YEAR	TEAM	LVL	AGE	PA	R	2B	3B	HR	RBI	BB	K	SB	CS	AVG/OBP/SLG
2018	ROM	LO-A	20	342	54	17	1	11	39	29	73	1	1	.293/.360/.463
2018	FLO	HI-A	20	90	3	7	0	0	10	6	16	0	0	.253/.300/.337
2019	FLO	HI-A	21	207	26	11	0	3	22	14	44	0	0	.263/.324/.368
2019	MIS	AA	21	209	24	9	0	3	17	15	40	0	0	.246/.306/.340
2020	ATL	MLB	22	10	0	1	0	0	1	0	4	0	0	.400/.400/.500
2021 FS	ATL	MLB	23	600	66	23	1	15	62	39	167	0	1	.226/.281/.359
2021 DC	ATL	MLB	23	120	13	4	0	3	12	7	33	0	0	.226/.281/.359

Comparables: Bryan Anderson, Austin Romine, Miguel Perez

YEAR	TEAM	P. COUNT	FRM RUNS	BLK RUNS	THRW RUNS	TOT RUNS
2020	ATL	404	0.0	0.0	0.0	0.0
2021	ATL	4810	-0.6	-0.3	0.0	-0.9
2021	ATL	4810	-0.6	-0.6	0.0	-1.2

Willson's little brother remains one of the more intriguing catching prospects in baseball, but without a minor league season to show off his stuff, he spent most of the year at the Braves' alternate site. He did get to make his MLB debut, though his time in the majors amounted to all of 10 plate appearances over four games in late July while Travis d'Arnaud and Tyler Flowers were both unavailable. The strong work of those two kept Contreras from claiming any larger role in Atlanta, but his time is coming: Flowers is a free agent this winter, and d'Arnaud has just one year left on his contract.

YEAR	TEAM	LVL	AGE	PA	DRC+	BABIP	BRR	FRAA	WARP
2018	ROM	LO-A	20	342	134	.351	-0.9	C(43): -0.3	1.6
2018	FLO	HI-A	20	90	102	.309	-0.3	C(20): -0.4	0.1
2019	FLO	HI-A	21	207	112	.329	-0.2	C(43): -0.8	1.0
2019	MIS	AA	21	209	99	.295	0.8	C(53): -1.1	0.9
2020	ATL	MLB	22	10	83	.667	-0.3	C(4): 0.2	0.0
2021 FS	ATL	MLB	23	600	77	.293	-0.8	C -3	0.3
2021 DC	ATL	MLB	23	120	77	.293	-0.2	C -1	0.0

Travis Demeritte LF
Born: 09/30/94   Age: 26   Bats: R   Throws: R
Height: 6'0"   Weight: 180   Origin: Round 1, 2013 Draft (#30 overall)

YEAR	TEAM	LVL	AGE	PA	R	2B	3B	HR	RBI	BB	K	SB	CS	AVG/OBP/SLG
2018	MIS	AA	23	494	69	22	5	17	63	57	140	6	2	.222/.316/.416
2019	GWN	AAA	24	399	68	28	2	20	73	51	106	4	3	.286/.387/.558
2019	DET	MLB	24	186	24	7	2	3	10	14	63	3	0	.225/.286/.343
2020	DET	MLB	25	33	5	1	0	0	4	3	14	0	0	.172/.273/.207
2021 FS	ATL	MLB	26	600	58	21	5	18	64	55	232	2	2	.194/.274/.355

Comparables: Joe Borchard, Doug Frobel, Jason Repko

Best-case scenario for Demeritte: He finally realizes his power potential and sticks around as a fourth outfielder, pinch hitting in the eighth inning of three-run deficits and leaving them untouched. Worst case: He keeps going down to Triple-A, falling victim to the easiest surname play on words in transaction history.

YEAR	TEAM	LVL	AGE	PA	DRC+	BABIP	BRR	FRAA	WARP
2018	MIS	AA	23	494	102	.284	-2.2	LF(119): -5.9, 3B(1): 0.1, CF(1): -0.2	-0.5
2019	GWN	AAA	24	399	136	.358	0.0	LF(38): 0.1, RF(36): -2.0	2.3
2019	DET	MLB	24	186	61	.337	1.7	RF(47): 3.8	0.0
2020	DET	MLB	25	33	63	.333	0.2	RF(12): 0.6, LF(2): 0.5, P(1): -0.0	0.0
2021 FS	ATL	MLB	26	600	73	.298	0.1	LF 0, RF 1	-0.5

Tyler Flowers   C

Born: 01/24/86   Age: 35   Bats: R   Throws: R
Height: 6'4"   Weight: 260   Origin: Round 33, 2005 Draft (#1007 overall)

YEAR	TEAM	LVL	AGE	PA	R	2B	3B	HR	RBI	BB	K	SB	CS	AVG/OBP/SLG
2018	ATL	MLB	32	296	34	9	0	8	30	35	76	0	0	.227/.341/.359
2019	ATL	MLB	33	310	36	11	3	11	34	31	105	0	0	.229/.319/.413
2020	ATL	MLB	34	80	5	6	0	1	5	8	34	0	0	.217/.325/.348
2021 FS	ATL	MLB	35	600	62	19	1	16	63	54	208	0	1	.210/.308/.351

Comparables: David Ross, Jason LaRue, Todd Pratt

Flowers' unexpected 2017 breakout continues to recede further and further into the distance, as his offense never found that level again and, in some cases, hit new lows, like a grotesque 42.5 percent strikeout rate. Entering 2021, it'd be pointless to expect anything more of Flowers than backup catcher-level offense, because, well, that's what he is: a backup catcher, and a glove-first one at that. The good thing for Flowers is that his blocking, framing and pitch-calling skills all remain above average, and as his skill with the bat decays, the average offensive production of catchers leaguewide plummets to match it. He should always be able to find a home as a clubhouse leader who can make a couple of starts a week, work with a young pitcher and run into a fastball every now and then.

YEAR	TEAM	P. COUNT	FRM RUNS	BLK RUNS	THRW RUNS	TOT RUNS
2018	ATL	10295	13.7	-0.4	-0.2	13.1
2019	ATL	11730	15.3	-3.8	-0.6	11.0
2020	ATL	3036	1.6	0.0	0.1	1.7
2021	ATL	16650	20.2	1.0	-0.4	20.7
2021	ATL	16650	20.2	-1.5	-0.4	18.2

YEAR	TEAM	LVL	AGE	PA	DRC+	BABIP	BRR	FRAA	WARP
2018	ATL	MLB	32	296	100	.292	0.3	C(76): 13.2	2.9
2019	ATL	MLB	33	310	79	.325	-3.7	C(83): 10.3	1.4
2020	ATL	MLB	34	80	73	.412	0.7	C(22): -0.1	0.2
2021 FS	ATL	MLB	35	600	86	.310	-0.8	C 18	3.2

Atlanta Braves 2021

Adeiny Hechavarría 2B
Born: 04/15/89 Age: 32 Bats: R Throws: R
Height: 6'0" Weight: 195 Origin: International Free Agent, 2010

YEAR	TEAM	LVL	AGE	PA	R	2B	3B	HR	RBI	BB	K	SB	CS	AVG/OBP/SLG
2018	NYY	MLB	29	37	3	0	0	2	2	1	10	1	0	.194/.216/.361
2018	TB	MLB	29	237	29	7	0	3	26	12	37	1	0	.258/.289/.332
2018	PIT	MLB	29	47	2	4	0	1	3	3	11	0	0	.233/.277/.395
2019	SYR	AAA	30	102	15	9	0	0	17	6	14	2	1	.348/.382/.446
2019	ATL	MLB	30	70	14	5	1	4	15	6	15	0	0	.328/.400/.639
2019	NYM	MLB	30	151	20	7	0	5	18	8	33	3	1	.204/.252/.359
2020	ATL	MLB	31	63	7	3	0	0	2	4	12	0	0	.254/.302/.305
2021 FS	ATL	MLB	32	600	54	25	2	12	60	35	120	3	2	.240/.288/.363

Comparables: Kiko Garcia, Bill Almon, Curtis Wilkerson

Hechavarría would've been perfectly at home in the 1970s as one of the decade's many all-glove infielders, a society of men whose on-base percentage and slugging percentage both floated in the low .300s. He's no fit at all for this modern era that requires you to, you know, hit.

YEAR	TEAM	LVL	AGE	PA	DRC+	BABIP	BRR	FRAA	WARP
2018	NYY	MLB	29	37	88	.208	0.1	SS(16): -1.4, 3B(4): -0.3	-0.1
2018	TB	MLB	29	237	88	.290	1.5	SS(61): -1.3	0.8
2018	PIT	MLB	29	47	87	.281	-1.3	SS(15): -1.1	-0.1
2019	SYR	AAA	30	102	122	.395	0.3	SS(14): 1.9, 3B(13): -1.1, 2B(2): 0.3	0.8
2019	ATL	MLB	30	70	132	.372	0.4	SS(12): -0.2, 2B(3): -0.4, 3B(1): -0.1	0.6
2019	NYM	MLB	30	151	72	.231	-1.8	2B(26): -1.6, SS(15): -0.2, 3B(8): -0.6	-0.4
2020	ATL	MLB	31	63	81	.319	-1.0	2B(12): -0.4, 3B(8): -0.4, SS(4): 0.0	-0.2
2021 FS	ATL	MLB	32	600	78	.283	-0.3	SS -1, 2B -1	-0.2

Alex Jackson C
Born: 12/25/95 Age: 25 Bats: R Throws: R
Height: 6'2" Weight: 215 Origin: Round 1, 2014 Draft (#6 overall)

YEAR	TEAM	LVL	AGE	PA	R	2B	3B	HR	RBI	BB	K	SB	CS	AVG/OBP/SLG
2018	MIS	AA	22	252	27	12	1	5	24	20	78	0	0	.200/.282/.329
2018	GWN	AAA	22	125	15	11	2	3	17	12	42	0	0	.204/.296/.426
2019	GWN	AAA	23	345	52	9	0	28	65	20	118	1	0	.229/.313/.533
2019	ATL	MLB	23	15	0	0	0	0	0	1	5	0	0	.000/.133/.000
2020	ATL	MLB	24	7	0	1	0	0	0	0	4	0	0	.286/.286/.429
2021 FS	ATL	MLB	25	600	65	17	1	17	59	38	233	0	0	.178/.255/.314
2021 DC	ATL	MLB	25	151	16	4	0	4	14	9	58	0	0	.178/.255/.314

Comparables: Kyle Skipworth, Greg Halman, Pete Alonso

Like fellow catching prospect Contreras, Jackson lost some sorely-needed reps last summer, hanging out at the Braves' alternate site aside from three days in late July and two in late August with the big club. What strides he made weren't documented, but the

YEAR	TEAM	P. COUNT	FRM RUNS	BLK RUNS	THRW RUNS	TOT RUNS
2019	ATL	534	0.3	0.1		0.4
2020	ATL	332	-0.1	0.0	0.0	-0.1
2021	ATL	6012	-1.2	0.4	0.2	-0.5
2021	ATL	6012	-1.2	0.7	0.2	-0.3

safe bet is that Atlanta focused on his bat-to-ball skills and his plate discipline, the two bugaboos in his game. The power, though, is there, and while he's a safer bet to spend 2021 in the minors than with the Braves, the world will always welcome both lovers and backup catchers who can swat.

YEAR	TEAM	LVL	AGE	PA	DRC+	BABIP	BRR	FRAA	WARP
2018	MIS	AA	22	252	69	.280	-0.9	C(61): -2.1	-0.4
2018	GWN	AAA	22	125	86	.292	0.2	C(29): 2.7	0.5
2019	GWN	AAA	23	345	105	.261	-2.8	C(78): 17.9	3.1
2019	ATL	MLB	23	15	76	.000		C(4): 0.5	0.1
2020	ATL	MLB	24	7	68	.667	-0.2	C(4): -0.0	0.0
2021 FS	ATL	MLB	25	600	59	.269	-0.7	C -2	-1.0
2021 DC	ATL	MLB	25	151	59	.269	-0.2	C -1	-0.3

Jason Kipnis 2B
Born: 04/03/87 Age: 34 Bats: L Throws: R
Height: 5'11" Weight: 200 Origin: Round 2, 2009 Draft (#63 overall)

YEAR	TEAM	LVL	AGE	PA	R	2B	3B	HR	RBI	BB	K	SB	CS	AVG/OBP/SLG
2018	CLE	MLB	31	601	65	28	1	18	75	60	112	7	1	.230/.315/.389
2019	CLE	MLB	32	511	52	23	1	17	65	40	88	7	2	.245/.304/.410
2020	CHC	MLB	33	135	13	8	1	3	16	18	41	1	0	.237/.341/.404
2021 FS	ATL	MLB	34	600	61	24	2	17	65	57	153	9	3	.213/.297/.367

Comparables: Tadahito Iguchi, Neil Walker, Brian Dozier

Throughout Kipnis' career, announcers have gotten a lot of mileage out of him hailing from Northbrook, Illinois. Kipnis' decision to join the Cubs allowed for that tattered fun fact to be repaired in the form of a "hometown kid" narrative. The more important thing to know here is that, while he finished with an OPS just under the league-average mark, his underlying metrics weren't supportive of his resurgence. Now entering his age-34 season, Kipnis is closer to joining a television booth and picking his own low-hanging biographical fruit than he is to returning to his past All-Star heights.

Atlanta Braves 2021

YEAR	TEAM	LVL	AGE	PA	DRC+	BABIP	BRR	FRAA	WARP
2018	CLE	MLB	31	601	93	.258	-1.2	2B(131): -0.5, CF(14): -2.0	1.1
2019	CLE	MLB	32	511	93	.265	0.2	2B(117): -0.0	1.3
2020	CHC	MLB	33	135	88	.333	-0.1	2B(36): 0.6, 1B(1): -0.1	0.3
2021 FS	ATL	MLB	34	600	82	.264	0.3	2B 0, CF -1	0.4

Shea Langeliers C
Born: 11/18/97   Age: 23   Bats: R   Throws: R
Height: 6'0"   Weight: 205   Origin: Round 1, 2019 Draft (#9 overall)

YEAR	TEAM	LVL	AGE	PA	R	2B	3B	HR	RBI	BB	K	SB	CS	AVG/OBP/SLG
2019	ROM	LO-A	21	239	27	13	0	2	34	17	55	0	0	.255/.310/.343
2021 FS	ATL	MLB	23	600	46	21	1	8	49	38	190	0	1	.195/.251/.288

Comparables: Josh Phegley, José Briceño, Kyle Higashioka

For as much as everyone talks about the Braves growing pitching prospects on trees, they're equally flush in catching talent. Langeliers is the best defender of the bunch and good enough to catch in the majors right now. He is not good enough to DH in the majors right now, as his stat line proves, but he has an excess of raw power to tap into as he climbs the proverbial ladder. The defense and leadership skills alone make Langeliers and his Zane Grey-caliber name one of the safest prospects in the low minors to bet on, but the bat may take a while.

YEAR	TEAM	LVL	AGE	PA	DRC+	BABIP	BRR	FRAA	WARP
2019	ROM	LO-A	21	239	100	.325	-1.3	C(42): 0.8	0.9
2021 FS	ATL	MLB	23	600	50	.278	-0.7	C 1	-1.3

Jack Mayfield 2B
Born: 09/30/90   Age: 30   Bats: R   Throws: R
Height: 5'11"   Weight: 190   Origin: Undrafted Free Agent, 2013

YEAR	TEAM	LVL	AGE	PA	R	2B	3B	HR	RBI	BB	K	SB	CS	AVG/OBP/SLG
2018	FRE	AAA	27	479	66	31	1	16	66	33	92	5	4	.270/.324/.457
2019	RR	AAA	28	431	78	26	1	26	79	37	78	7	1	.287/.350/.566
2019	HOU	MLB	28	65	8	5	0	2	5	1	16	0	0	.156/.169/.328
2020	HOU	MLB	29	47	5	1	0	0	3	2	14	0	0	.190/.239/.214
2021 FS	ATL	MLB	30	600	70	23	1	22	74	38	165	0	1	.215/.272/.383
2021 DC	ATL	MLB	30	60	7	2	0	2	7	2	16	0	0	.215/.272/.383

Comparables: Josh Barfield, Chris Valaika, Whit Merrifield

Mayfield is an unfortunate surname for a baseball player. Something definitive like Jack Willfield would be more reassuring. Nominative determinism aside, it turns out that Jack can field but can't hit, at least at the major-league level. He should return to producing above-average slash lines at Triple-A with the occasional foray onto the big-league bench.

YEAR	TEAM	LVL	AGE	PA	DRC+	BABIP	BRR	FRAA	WARP
2018	FRE	AAA	27	479	109	.304	-0.2	2B(62): -6.3, SS(48): -8.9, 3B(4): -0.7	0.1
2019	RR	AAA	28	431	117	.291	0.0	SS(43): -1.5, 2B(33): 2.9, 3B(24): -1.5	2.5
2019	HOU	MLB	28	65	72	.174	-0.6	SS(21): 0.2, 2B(5): -0.2, 3B(1): -0.0	0.0
2020	HOU	MLB	29	47	66	.276	-0.1	3B(8): 0.4, SS(8): -0.5, 2B(5): -0.1	-0.2
2021 FS	ATL	MLB	30	600	78	.262	-0.8	SS -3, 2B -1	-0.4
2021 DC	ATL	MLB	30	60	78	.262	-0.1	SS 0, 2B 0	0.0

Cristian Pache CF

Born: 11/19/98 Age: 22 Bats: R Throws: R
Height: 6'2" Weight: 215 Origin: International Free Agent, 2015

YEAR	TEAM	LVL	AGE	PA	R	2B	3B	HR	RBI	BB	K	SB	CS	AVG/OBP/SLG
2018	FLO	HI-A	19	387	46	20	5	8	40	15	69	7	6	.285/.311/.431
2018	MIS	AA	19	109	10	3	1	1	7	5	28	0	2	.260/.294/.337
2019	MIS	AA	20	433	50	28	8	11	53	34	104	8	11	.278/.340/.474
2019	GWN	AAA	20	105	13	8	1	1	8	9	18	0	0	.274/.337/.411
2020	ATL	MLB	21	4	0	0	0	0	0	0	2	0	0	.250/.250/.250
2021 FS	ATL	MLB	22	600	65	18	5	13	64	36	160	9	6	.233/.282/.361
2021 DC	ATL	MLB	22	480	52	14	4	10	51	28	128	7	5	.233/.282/.361

Comparables: Felix Pie, Greg Halman, Anthony Gose

The man (barely; he just turned 22 in November) atop Atlanta's prospect lists got more playing time in October than the regular season, as Pache was thrust into action after Adam Duvall pulled an oblique in Game 1 of the NLCS. He quickly showed just why scouts and analysts alike have drooled over him, displaying dizzying speed on the bases and elite defense in center field. It's the offense that still needs the most work: Pache has yet to display much if any power and has a ways to go with his selectivity. If nothing else, though, the defense is enough to make him a regular. Barring some surprise (or some unsurprising service time manipulation), he'll be on the Opening Day roster and a starter in his own right.

YEAR	TEAM	LVL	AGE	PA	DRC+	BABIP	BRR	FRAA	WARP
2018	FLO	HI-A	19	387	113	.330	-1.1	CF(93): 3.9	1.3
2018	MIS	AA	19	109	71	.347	-0.5	CF(28): 1.3	-0.1
2019	MIS	AA	20	433	139	.351	-1.7	CF(58): 1.6, RF(23): 3.3, LF(22): 0.0	3.3
2019	GWN	AAA	20	105	90	.329	-0.9	CF(23): -3.2, RF(3): 3.3	0.2
2020	ATL	MLB	21	4	83	.500		LF(2): 0.2	0.0
2021 FS	ATL	MLB	22	600	75	.302	1.3	CF 4, LF 0	0.5
2021 DC	ATL	MLB	22	480	75	.302	1.1	CF 3	0.5

Atlanta Braves 2021

Mel Rojas Jr. CF
Born: 05/24/90 Age: 31 Bats: S Throws: R
Height: 6'2" Weight: 225 Origin: Round 3, 2010 Draft (#84 overall)

YEAR	TEAM	LVL	AGE	PA	R	2B	3B	HR	RBI	BB	K	SB	CS	AVG/OBP/SLG
2018	KT	KBO	28	645	114	30	1	43	114	71	142	18	13	.305/.388/.590
2019	KT	KBO	29	578	68	30	3	24	104	49	120	4	4	.322/.381/.530
2020	KT	KBO	30	628	116	39	1	47	135	65	132	0	1	.349/.417/.680
2021								No projection						

While all international players in the KBO must constantly decide whether to remain large fish in a small pond, the choice Rojas faced must have felt particularly agonizing. On the one hand, he's done just about all he can do in the KBO. Rojas came within a whisker of the Triple Crown in 2020 and easily won the league's MVP. In Suwon, he's a club legend and the franchise's best ever player. He's 30 now, and as one of the only foreign players in the league without MLB experience, one imagines that he was sorely tempted by the chance to play in the majors. Major league clubs were poking around, and there's no reason to think he couldn't have parlayed his big numbers into a one-year deal and perhaps a seven-figure salary.

At the same time, Rojas's game is not likely to translate all that well. The logical comparison is Eric Thames, and while Thames has enjoyed some success since returning stateside, he also has more raw power and a significantly better eye than Rojas. Perhaps Mel Jr. would be content to be the lite version of Eric Thames and take a job as someone's fourth or fifth outfielder. Then again, maybe not. To watch Rojas last year was to watch a man on top of the world. On the field and in the dugout he radiates joy, and he takes an obvious pride in being KT's talisman. It seems like an awful lot to give up just to become another cog in MLB's machine. And yet he opted for a third path, splitting the difference, signing a two-year, $5 million contract to join the Hanshin Tigers of the NPB.

YEAR	TEAM	LVL	AGE	PA	DRC+	BABIP	BRR	FRAA	WARP
2018	KT	KBO	28	645					
2019	KT	KBO	29	578					
2020	KT	KBO	30	628					
2021					No projection				

Pablo Sandoval 3B

Born: 08/11/86 Age: 34 Bats: S Throws: R
Height: 5'10" Weight: 268 Origin: International Free Agent, 2003

YEAR	TEAM	LVL	AGE	PA	R	2B	3B	HR	RBI	BB	K	SB	CS	AVG/OBP/SLG
2018	SF	MLB	31	252	22	10	1	9	40	19	52	0	0	.248/.310/.417
2019	SF	MLB	32	296	42	23	0	14	41	18	67	1	0	.268/.313/.507
2020	SF	MLB	33	90	5	1	0	1	6	6	18	0	0	.220/.278/.268
2020	ATL	MLB	33	4	0	0	0	0	0	2	1	0	0	.000/.500/.000
2021 FS	ATL	MLB	34	600	60	23	1	18	67	40	135	1	1	.226/.285/.378

Comparables: Adrián Beltré, Sean Berry, Tim Wallach

For all of the imperfections in Sandoval's game, getting bat to ball—whether at eye- or shoetop-level—was both his calling card and *raison d'être*. With that skill in free-fall, there seems little left to sustain a relatively brief, but extremely storied, career. His three-homer World Series Game One against the Tigers in 2012 and his 2014 World Series-clinching catch, plopping on his backside in foul ground with Sal Perez's popout safely stowed, remain the Panda's iconic moments. The fact that he may have played his final postseason in an Atlanta uniform will be the answer to a trivia question decades hence, but no matter his past, present, or future shape, he'll always be a Giant.

YEAR	TEAM	LVL	AGE	PA	DRC+	BABIP	BRR	FRAA	WARP
2018	SF	MLB	31	252	95	.282	-2.8	3B(36): -1.8, 1B(24): -1.4, 2B(2): -0.6	-0.1
2019	SF	MLB	32	296	97	.304	0.0	3B(45): -4.1, 1B(23): 0.1, P(1): -0.0	0.4
2020	SF	MLB	33	90	82	.266	-0.5	1B(8): 0.3, 3B(4): -0.3	-0.1
2020	ATL	MLB	33	4		.000	0.0	3B(1): 0.1	
2021 FS	ATL	MLB	34	600	83	.265	-0.7	3B -4, 1B 0	-0.8

Braden Shewmake SS
Born: 11/19/97 Age: 23 Bats: L Throws: R
Height: 6'4" Weight: 190 Origin: Round 1, 2019 Draft (#21 overall)

YEAR	TEAM	LVL	AGE	PA	R	2B	3B	HR	RBI	BB	K	SB	CS	AVG/OBP/SLG
2019	ROM	LO-A	21	226	37	18	2	3	39	21	29	11	3	.318/.389/.473
2019	MIS	AA	21	52	7	0	0	0	1	4	11	2	0	.217/.288/.217
2021 FS	ATL	MLB	23	600	52	25	2	10	55	38	141	10	3	.226/.284/.339

Comparables: Max Schrock, Stephen Piscotty, Garin Cecchini

Atlanta's first-round pick in 2019 tore up Low-A before a brief yet rocky stint in Double-A, but with no minor league season in '20, Shewmake was left to continue his development away from the prying eyes of scouts and analysts. What he showed in his draft summer at the plate and in the field was enough to get him into the Braves' Top 10 list; the trick will be developing power and showing enough offense to keep that spot in a deep and competitive system and escape a future as a utility player. Well, that and finding the missing R from his last name.

YEAR	TEAM	LVL	AGE	PA	DRC+	BABIP	BRR	FRAA	WARP
2019	ROM	LO-A	21	226	162	.359	3.5	SS(39): -0.0	2.5
2019	MIS	AA	21	52	58	.278	0.7	SS(14): 1.8	0.3
2021 FS	ATL	MLB	23	600	72	.285	0.4	SS 5	0.3

Drew Waters CF

Born: 12/30/98 Age: 22 Bats: S Throws: R
Height: 6'2" Weight: 185 Origin: Round 2, 2017 Draft (#41 overall)

YEAR	TEAM	LVL	AGE	PA	R	2B	3B	HR	RBI	BB	K	SB	CS	AVG/OBP/SLG
2018	ROM	LO-A	19	365	58	32	6	9	36	21	72	20	5	.303/.353/.513
2018	FLO	HI-A	19	133	14	7	3	0	3	8	33	3	0	.268/.316/.374
2019	MIS	AA	20	454	63	35	9	5	41	28	121	13	6	.319/.366/.481
2019	GWN	AAA	20	119	17	5	0	2	11	11	43	3	0	.271/.336/.374
2021 FS	ATL	MLB	22	600	63	22	4	11	62	37	209	8	3	.213/.268/.335
2021 DC	ATL	MLB	22	200	21	7	1	3	20	12	69	2	1	.213/.268/.335

Comparables: Cristian Pache, Felix Pie, Fernando Tatis Jr.

The other precocious outfielder in Atlanta's system, Waters offers more offensive upside than Pache, but is a step down in terms of defense and also carries a ton of swing-and-miss in his game. That plate discipline will be the deciding factor as to whether Waters is a first-division regular or a guy who bounces around the league as a toolsy reserve who can't quite put it all together. His glove and his speed are enough to contend for a bench spot now, if nothing else. Like everyone else in the Braves' system, he's preposterously young, and there's still plenty of time to develop. If and when that time comes, he, Pache and Acuña are going to make for an outfield where no ball falls in and one that leads the league in panache.

YEAR	TEAM	LVL	AGE	PA	DRC+	BABIP	BRR	FRAA	WARP
2018	ROM	LO-A	19	365	139	.362	3.9	CF(83): -0.6	2.4
2018	FLO	HI-A	19	133	92	.363	0.0	CF(30): -1.5, RF(1): -0.1	-0.1
2019	MIS	AA	20	454	143	.436	-3.3	LF(55): 6.3, CF(38): 7.0, RF(18): -1.2	4.2
2019	GWN	AAA	20	119	79	.429	0.7	RF(16): 2.1, LF(7): 0.4, CF(3): 0.8	0.3
2021 FS	ATL	MLB	22	600	65	.317	0.8	LF 11, RF 2	0.5
2021 DC	ATL	MLB	22	200	65	.317	0.3	LF 4, RF 1	0.0

Victor Arano RHP
Born: 02/07/95 Age: 26 Bats: R Throws: R
Height: 6'2" Weight: 228 Origin: International Free Agent, 2013

YEAR	TEAM	LVL	AGE	W	L	SV	G	GS	IP	H	HR	BB/9	K/9	K	GB%	BABIP
2018	PHI	MLB	23	1	2	3	60	0	59^1	54	6	2.6	9.1	60	38.7%	.296
2019	PHI	MLB	24	1	0	0	3	0	4^2	2	1	3.9	13.5	7	28.6%	.167
2021 FS	ATL	MLB	26	2	2	0	57	0	50	43	6	4.0	10.2	56	38.4%	.287
2021 DC	ATL	MLB	26	2	2	0	40	0	30.3	26	4	4.0	10.2	34	38.4%	.287

Comparables: Roberto Osuna, Paco Rodríguez, Keynan Middleton

The idea of a second spring training must have been terrifying to Arano, who strained his shoulder the first time around and spent the rest of the year, summer camp included, not quite getting back up to speed. Having lost most of 2019 to bone spurs, the fastball-slider reliever will enter next spring as a bit of a forgotten man; given what transpired to the corps in his absence, the anonymity could work to his advantage.

YEAR	TEAM	LVL	AGE	WHIP	ERA	DRA-	WARP	MPH	FB%	WHF	CSP
2018	PHI	MLB	23	1.20	2.73	79	0.9	95.7	40.4%	32.2%	
2019	PHI	MLB	24	0.86	3.86	102	0.0	96.0	38.8%	51.4%	
2021 FS	ATL	MLB	26	1.31	3.79	91	0.5	95.8	40.2%	34.6%	44.7%
2021 DC	ATL	MLB	26	1.31	3.79	91	0.3	95.8	40.2%	34.6%	44.7%

Tucker Davidson LHP
Born: 03/25/96 Age: 25 Bats: L Throws: L
Height: 6'2" Weight: 215 Origin: Round 19, 2016 Draft (#559 overall)

YEAR	TEAM	LVL	AGE	W	L	SV	G	GS	IP	H	HR	BB/9	K/9	K	GB%	BABIP
2018	FLO	HI-A	22	7	10	0	24	24	118^1	120	5	4.4	7.5	99	46.7%	.334
2019	MIS	AA	23	7	6	0	21	21	110^2	88	5	3.7	9.9	122	48.6%	.311
2019	GWN	AAA	23	1	1	0	4	4	19	20	0	4.3	5.7	12	49.2%	.345
2020	ATL	MLB	24	0	1	0	1	1	1^2	3	1	21.6	10.8	2	28.6%	.333
2021 FS	ATL	MLB	25	2	3	0	57	0	50	48	7	5.3	8.2	45	45.6%	.291
2021 DC	ATL	MLB	25	1	1	0	4	4	19.3	18	2	5.3	8.2	17	45.6%	.291

Comparables: Bernardo Flores Jr., Robert Dugger, Ryan Helsley

Davidson is no leviathan, but Thomas Hobbes nailed his MLB debut: nasty, brutish and short. He remains one of Atlanta's top pitching prospects, though, thanks to premium velocity and a high-spin curveball.

YEAR	TEAM	LVL	AGE	WHIP	ERA	DRA-	WARP	MPH	FB%	WHF	CSP
2018	FLO	HI-A	22	1.50	4.18	91	1.2				
2019	MIS	AA	23	1.20	2.03	91	0.7				
2019	GWN	AAA	23	1.53	2.84	112	0.2				
2020	ATL	MLB	24	4.20	10.80	119	0.0	93.9	75.5%	16.7%	
2021 FS	ATL	MLB	25	1.57	5.05	113	-0.1	93.9	75.5%	16.7%	42.0%
2021 DC	ATL	MLB	25	1.57	5.05	113	0.0	93.9	75.5%	16.7%	42.0%

Jasseel De La Cruz RHP

Born: 06/26/97   Age: 24   Bats: R   Throws: R
Height: 6'1"   Weight: 195   Origin: International Free Agent, 2015

YEAR	TEAM	LVL	AGE	W	L	SV	G	GS	IP	H	HR	BB/9	K/9	K	GB%	BABIP
2018	ROM	LO-A	21	3	4	0	15	13	69	65	6	4.4	8.5	65	62.4%	.309
2019	ROM	LO-A	22	0	1	0	4	4	18	19	1	2.5	11.0	22	51.1%	.391
2019	FLO	HI-A	22	3	1	0	4	4	28	12	0	2.2	8.4	26	52.2%	.174
2019	MIS	AA	22	4	7	0	17	16	87	71	7	3.8	7.6	73	45.4%	.263
2021 FS	ATL	MLB	24	2	3	0	57	0	50	48	8	5.3	7.9	43	42.4%	.284
2021 DC	ATL	MLB	24	0	0	0	11	0	12	11	1	5.3	7.9	10	42.4%	.284

Comparables: Chad Bettis, Braden Shipley, John Gant

A live-armed righty with control issues, De La Cruz never got a chance to show his stuff in Atlanta after a solid 2019 despite being on the team's 40-man roster, spending all summer at the Braves' alternate site. A strong spring training likely lands him in the Opening Day bullpen.

YEAR	TEAM	LVL	AGE	WHIP	ERA	DRA-	WARP	MPH	FB%	WHF	CSP
2018	ROM	LO-A	21	1.43	4.83	88	0.8				
2019	ROM	LO-A	22	1.33	2.50	96	0.1				
2019	FLO	HI-A	22	0.68	1.93	50	0.9				
2019	MIS	AA	22	1.24	3.83	96	0.3				
2021 FS	ATL	MLB	24	1.57	5.24	119	-0.3				
2021 DC	ATL	MLB	24	1.57	5.24	119	-0.1				

Carl Edwards Jr.   RHP
Born: 09/03/91   Age: 29   Bats: R   Throws: R
Height: 6'3"   Weight: 170   Origin: Round 48, 2011 Draft (#1464 overall)

YEAR	TEAM	LVL	AGE	W	L	SV	G	GS	IP	H	HR	BB/9	K/9	K	GB%	BABIP
2018	CHC	MLB	26	3	2	0	58	0	52	36	2	5.5	11.6	67	30.9%	.283
2019	IOW	AAA	27	2	0	0	14	0	14²	12	2	3.7	8.6	14	54.8%	.250
2019	SD	MLB	27	0	0	0	2	0	1²	4	0	21.6	10.8	2	37.5%	.500
2019	CHC	MLB	27	1	1	0	20	0	15¹	8	3	5.3	10.0	17	24.3%	.147
2020	SEA	MLB	28	0	0	1	5	0	4²	2	0	1.9	11.6	6	60.0%	.200
2021 FS	ATL	MLB	29	2	2	0	57	0	50	39	5	5.7	11.0	60	40.1%	.282

Comparables: Dominic Leone, Ken Giles, Arodys Vizcaíno

Edwards came into 2020 needing to prove he could command his quality, high-velocity fastball well enough to put some of the shine back on what was once a promising relief career. Despite an encouraging handful of appearances before a forearm strain cut the short season shorter, it's hard to think much of that changed. For now, Edwards will have to add "staying healthy" to an already long list of things he needs to prove to recapture his career's momentum. The stuff is willing, but the circumstances have been finicky.

YEAR	TEAM	LVL	AGE	WHIP	ERA	DRA-	WARP	MPH	FB%	WHF	CSP
2018	CHC	MLB	26	1.31	2.60	98	0.3	96.3	75.8%	33.5%	
2019	IOW	AAA	27	1.23	3.07	69	0.4				
2019	SD	MLB	27	4.80	32.40	76	0.0	95.5	66.7%	30.4%	
2019	CHC	MLB	27	1.11	5.87	112	0.0	95.8	76.2%	21.6%	
2020	SEA	MLB	28	0.64	1.93	86	0.1	94.6	66.1%	41.7%	
2021 FS	ATL	MLB	29	1.41	3.99	88	0.6	95.9	74.5%	30.2%	44.5%

Cole Hamels LHP

Born: 12/27/83 Age: 37 Bats: L Throws: L
Height: 6'4" Weight: 205 Origin: Round 1, 2002 Draft (#17 overall)

YEAR	TEAM	LVL	AGE	W	L	SV	G	GS	IP	H	HR	BB/9	K/9	K	GB%	BABIP
2018	TEX	MLB	34	5	9	0	20	20	114^1	115	23	3.3	9.0	114	44.3%	.296
2018	CHC	MLB	34	4	3	0	12	12	76^1	61	6	2.7	8.7	74	46.2%	.288
2019	CHC	MLB	35	7	7	0	27	27	141^2	141	17	3.6	9.0	142	45.4%	.319
2020	ATL	MLB	36	0	1	0	1	1	3^1	3	0	2.7	5.4	2	36.4%	.273
2021 FS	ATL	MLB	37	9	9	0	26	26	150	146	22	4.1	8.6	143	44.8%	.294
2021 DC	ATL	MLB	37	6	6	0	20	20	100	97	15	4.1	8.6	95	44.8%	.294

Comparables: Zack Greinke, Aníbal Sánchez, Justin Verlander

All we saw and heard of Hamels in 2020—and likely the entirety of his Braves career—were intermittent appearances at training camp and one 3⅓ inning start in September. Tendinitis in his left triceps was the persistent bugaboo, and worrisomely, it morphed into shoulder fatigue that put an end to his season before it ever got a chance to begin. A full offseason of rest can only help, but at 37 years old and with stuff and peripherals on the decline, Hamels will have to prove he can handle the burdens of a rotation spot before he'll be given another one.

YEAR	TEAM	LVL	AGE	WHIP	ERA	DRA-	WARP	MPH	FB%	WHF	CSP
2018	TEX	MLB	34	1.37	4.72	115	0.2	93.4	60.3%	27.1%	
2018	CHC	MLB	34	1.10	2.36	77	1.6	94.5	67.8%	27.0%	
2019	CHC	MLB	35	1.39	3.81	99	1.4	93.0	66.3%	27.5%	
2020	ATL	MLB	36	1.20	8.10	124	0.0	90.3	55.8%	28.0%	
2021 FS	ATL	MLB	37	1.43	4.65	106	0.9	93.3	64.9%	27.4%	46.9%
2021 DC	ATL	MLB	37	1.43	4.65	106	0.6	93.3	64.9%	27.4%	46.9%

Kyle Muller LHP

Born: 10/07/97   Age: 23   Bats: R   Throws: L
Height: 6'7"   Weight: 250   Origin: Round 2, 2016 Draft (#44 overall)

YEAR	TEAM	LVL	AGE	W	L	SV	G	GS	IP	H	HR	BB/9	K/9	K	GB%	BABIP
2018	ROM	LO-A	20	3	0	0	6	6	30	24	3	2.4	6.9	23	50.0%	.256
2018	FLO	HI-A	20	4	2	0	14	14	80^2	80	2	3.6	8.8	79	39.6%	.355
2018	DAY	HI-A	20	2	0	0	2	2	13	10	0	2.8	11.1	16		.357
2018	MIS	AA	20	4	1	0	5	5	29	22	3	1.9	8.4	27	35.8%	.247
2019	MIS	AA	21	7	6	0	22	22	111^2	81	5	5.5	9.7	120	39.2%	.286
2021 FS	ATL	MLB	23	2	3	0	57	0	50	46	7	5.3	8.6	47	38.3%	.282
2021 DC	ATL	MLB	23	1	1	0	4	4	19.3	18	2	5.3	8.6	18	38.3%	.282

Comparables: Rony García, Luis Severino, Jayson Aquino

Part of the same draft class that produced Ian Anderson, Muller wasn't able to replicate his erstwhile teammate's major league success, remaining at the Braves' alternate site all summer. For most teams, the alternate site was a source of mystery, but with Atlanta bleeding out pitchers over the fall, any in-house option that failed to escape its gravitational pull has to be treated with some suspicion. Some daylight and game experience can only help the lefty on his quest to join the rotation alongside Anderson, as opposed to pre-2020 projections that had him in the bullpen long-term as a power arm from the left side.

YEAR	TEAM	LVL	AGE	WHIP	ERA	DRA-	WARP	MPH	FB%	WHF	CSP
2018	ROM	LO-A	20	1.07	2.40	99	0.2				
2018	FLO	HI-A	20	1.39	3.24	98	0.5				
2018	DAY	HI-A	20	1.08	0.00						
2018	MIS	AA	20	0.97	3.10	89	0.4				
2019	MIS	AA	21	1.33	3.14	99	0.1				
2021 FS	ATL	MLB	23	1.51	4.80	111	-0.1				
2021 DC	ATL	MLB	23	1.51	4.80	111	0.1				

Jared Shuster LHP

Born: 08/03/98   Age: 22   Bats: L   Throws: L
Height: 6'3"   Weight: 210   Origin: Round 1, 2020 Draft (#25 overall)

A somewhat underslot pick out of Wake Forest, Shuster employed a dominant 2019 stint in the Cape and a strong 2020 college season to force his way up draft boards. He found his way into the first round after looking good in four starts for the Demon Deacons before the college season came to an early end, showing improved velocity and stuff. The lefty's problem as a freshman and sophomore was walks—58 free passes in 102 innings over those two seasons—so it's encouraging to see that he handed out just five walks in seven starts in the Cape Cod League in 2019, then walked only four batters in 26⅓ innings in his final year at Wake Forest. Assuming the 2021 season is something closer to normal, he'll likely head to Single-A next spring to work on developing his secondary pitches and showing that his newfound control is no fluke.

Chad Sobotka RHP

Born: 07/10/93   Age: 27   Bats: R   Throws: R
Height: 6'7"   Weight: 225   Origin: Round 4, 2014 Draft (#133 overall)

YEAR	TEAM	LVL	AGE	W	L	SV	G	GS	IP	H	HR	BB/9	K/9	K	GB%	BABIP
2018	FLO	HI-A	24	2	0	2	13	1	20^1	9	0	3.1	12.4	28	37.5%	.225
2018	MIS	AA	24	2	3	6	22	0	28	16	1	4.2	11.9	37	30.0%	.259
2018	GWN	AAA	24	0	0	3	9	0	9^1	5	0	8.7	11.6	12	38.1%	.238
2018	ATL	MLB	24	1	0	0	14	0	14^1	5	2	5.7	13.2	21	28.6%	.120
2019	GWN	AAA	25	2	1	2	17	0	20^2	23	3	1.7	13.9	32	46.2%	.408
2019	ATL	MLB	25	0	0	0	32	0	29	28	6	5.9	11.8	38	44.6%	.324
2020	ATL	MLB	26	0	0	0	4	0	3^2	6	0	4.9	4.9	2	18.8%	.375
2021 FS	ATL	MLB	27	2	3	0	57	0	50	44	7	5.3	10.6	59	39.4%	.294
2021 DC	ATL	MLB	27	1	1	0	34	0	36.3	32	5	5.3	10.6	43	39.4%	.294

Comparables: Keynan Middleton, James Norwood, Edubray Ramos

Given that 2020 was a leap year, it's understandable that everyone might have one day they'd like to remove to return to a more standard 365. Sobotka would pick September 5, when he gave up five earned runs in two-thirds of an inning, moving his season ERA from a pristine 0.00 to 12.27. He didn't pitch again the rest of the way.

Atlanta Braves 2021

YEAR	TEAM	LVL	AGE	WHIP	ERA	DRA-	WARP	MPH	FB%	WHF	CSP
2018	FLO	HI-A	24	0.79	2.21	43	0.7				
2018	MIS	AA	24	1.04	1.93	45	0.9				
2018	GWN	AAA	24	1.50	1.93	75	0.1				
2018	ATL	MLB	24	0.98	1.88	53	0.4	98.1	63.6%	30.7%	
2019	GWN	AAA	25	1.31	4.79	64	0.6				
2019	ATL	MLB	25	1.62	6.21	92	0.3	97.9	56.6%	35.1%	
2020	ATL	MLB	26	2.18	12.27	131	0.0	96.1	62.5%	12.1%	
2021 FS	ATL	MLB	27	1.48	4.72	106	0.1	97.7	58.5%	31.0%	43.6%
2021 DC	ATL	MLB	27	1.48	4.72	106	0.0	97.7	58.5%	31.0%	43.6%

Patrick Weigel RHP
Born: 07/08/94   Age: 26   Bats: R   Throws: R
Height: 6'6"   Weight: 240   Origin: Round 7, 2015 Draft (#210 overall)

YEAR	TEAM	LVL	AGE	W	L	SV	G	GS	IP	H	HR	BB/9	K/9	K	GB%	BABIP
2018	BRA	ROK	23	0	0	0	4	3	4	2	0	0.0	13.5	6	33.3%	.333
2019	MIS	AA	24	0	1	0	7	7	15^2	8	0	5.2	9.2	16	53.8%	.205
2019	GWN	AAA	24	6	1	0	21	11	63^1	42	9	4.5	7.8	55	36.3%	.214
2020	ATL	MLB	25	0	0	0	1	0	0^2	2	0	40.5	0.0	0	25.0%	.500
2021 FS	ATL	MLB	26	2	3	0	57	0	50	49	8	5.0	8.4	46	39.7%	.290
2021 DC	ATL	MLB	26	2	1	0	18	1	24.7	24	4	5.0	8.4	23	39.7%	.290

Comparables: Ryan Helsley, Chase De Jong, Brady Lail

Tommy John surgery in 2017 couldn't slow Weigel, a fastball-slider righty who can touch 99 mph and generally sits 95. What has kept him in neutral is a total lack of control. Still, his 2020 easily beat his 2019, when he got called up to the bigs three different times without actually making it into a game.

YEAR	TEAM	LVL	AGE	WHIP	ERA	DRA-	WARP	MPH	FB%	WHF	CSP
2018	BRA	ROK	23	0.50	0.00						
2019	MIS	AA	24	1.09	1.72	66	0.3				
2019	GWN	AAA	24	1.17	2.98	62	2.2				
2020	ATL	MLB	25	7.50	27.00	99	0.0	95.6	58.3%	0.0%	
2021 FS	ATL	MLB	26	1.54	5.31	119	-0.3	95.6	58.3%	0.0%	43.6%
2021 DC	ATL	MLB	26	1.54	5.31	119	-0.1	95.6	58.3%	0.0%	43.6%

Braves Prospects

The State of the System:
There's still a few of the same names who have made this a perennial Top 10 system during their rebuild and contention cycle, but Atlanta is probably not long for the Top 10 of our org rankings. That doesn't really matter when you've won back-to-back division titles, and there are a few more bullets to fire here to get the big-league club over that last playoff hump.

The Top Ten:

1 — ★ ★ ★ *2021 Top 101 Prospect* #5 ★ ★ ★ —
Ian Anderson   RHP   OFP: 70   ETA: Debuted in 2020
Born: 05/02/98   Age: 23   Bats: R   Throws: R   Height: 6'3"   Weight: 170
Origin: Round 1, 2016 Draft (#3 overall)

The Report: Entering 2020, Anderson was an extremely good pitching prospect, straddling the 70/60 OFP border for the previous few years. He had a plus fastball and a plus curveball dating back to the draft, coming out of a difficult arm angle that was tough for hitters to pick up. The changeup flashed but lacked consistency, and the command sometimes wobbled. The statistical track record was solid outside of a late-season Triple-A stumble, but a lot of pitchers struggled in the 2019 Triple-A offensive barrage. In last year's *Annual* we wrote he was "a touch less likely to hit a top-of-the-rotation outcome (perhaps 20 percent instead of 25 percent) since he hasn't taken a major step forward in stuff and the command hasn't sharpened out yet." That "yet" is a saving grace.

Development Track: Anderson showed up in the majors on August 31 with everything he already had in the minors—along with one of the best changeups in baseball, fully formed, and improved command. Welp.

You probably know how the rest of this all went already. He was one of the best starting pitchers in baseball from his debut right through until Game 7 of the NLCS. Armed with his easy plus-plus change, he's now one of the best prospects in baseball. He's frankly more of a "young major-league star" in profile than a "prospect."

Variance: About as low as you can get for a pitcher. Anderson showed every indication he was already a present No. 2 starter in the majors this year, and he has no specific health or durability concerns. He's a hard 7 now.

Mark Barry's Fantasy Take: Unless your name rhymes with Mixto, I can't think of another pitching prospect who boosted his stock with a breathtaking late-season run more than Anderson. Heading into the season, I liked the strikeout potential, but was concerned about the walks/WHIP. After this season, I'm still slightly troubled by the walks, but Anderson showed that his stuff certainly plays against big-league hitters, so we're still in a better spot. Anderson is an SP2, and he'll flirt with SP1 seasons, especially if he masters the command.

★ ★ ★ *2021 Top 101 Prospect* **#18** ★ ★ ★

2 Cristian Pache CF   OFP: 70   ETA: Debuted in 2020
Born: 11/19/98   Age: 22   Bats: R   Throws: R   Height: 6'2"   Weight: 215
Origin: International Free Agent, 2015

The Report: Pache is an elite defensive center field prospect; extremely rangy with a plus-plus arm. When you start off a prospect evaluation with the defense, though, that in and of itself says something about the bat. We've been concerned about the swing-and-miss and approach issues for several years now, and we remain concerned. His walk rate improved in 2019 but not to the point of being outright good, and his strikeout rate ticked up too, especially at Double-A. He's grown into some power, so even without a big hit tool improvement he should provide offensive value, and he's made improvements to his swing that hint the big hit tool improvement may yet be coming. If he gets there, there's superstar potential.

Development Track: Entering the playoffs, we were a bit perplexed as to why we hadn't seen a lot of Pache during the 2020 season. He'd been sparingly used, appearing in only two games and both times he was in left field. Before we got a chance to really drill down into why he wasn't being used much, he was added to the playoff roster. After spending the first two rounds as a corner defensive replacement, he was inserted into the regular lineup in center for the NLCS when Adam Duvall got hurt. It was only 25 plate appearances, but he didn't look out of place.

Variance: Medium. His glove is likely to carry the profile some even if he doesn't hit a whole lot, but we don't actually have anyone on staff who is completely sold that he's going to hit a *whole* lot.

Mark Barry's Fantasy Take: Please stand by for the first of many "Better IRL than in fantasy" tags. Pache might be better IRL than in fantasy. When your A1 calling card is defense, that tends to be the case. Still, there's a lot to dream on with Pache's offensive profile. He brought some new and improved plate discipline to his brief stint with the big club down the stretch, and there's definitely speed, even if it hasn't consistently manifested on the bases. There's stuff to like, but it's still projection. If things break right, we could see .280ish with 15 homers and 20 steals, which isn't too shabby.

★ ★ ★ *2021 Top 101 Prospect* **#40** ★ ★ ★

3 **Drew Waters** CF   OFP: 60 ETA: 2021
Born: 12/30/98 Age: 22 Bats: S Throws: R Height: 6'2" Weight: 185
Origin: Round 2, 2017 Draft (#41 overall)

The Report: Waters has been on the fast track through the Braves' system since he was drafted in the second round in 2017. He has shown great offensive potential as a switch-hitter with above-average power potential, and has hit at every stop, capturing the Double-A Southern League batting title and MVP Award in 2019. Waters has a chance to be a perennial .300 hitter with 20-home run pop if his hyper-aggressive approach doesn't overwhelm his natural bat-to-ball abilities. He's a solid center fielder, but not good enough to displace Pache. Very few prospects would be, though.

Development Track: The lack of a minor league season in 2020 denied Waters an opportunity to further his offensive development against upper-level pitchers. He has just 119 plate appearances at the Triple-A level and the Braves have no need to rush him. Waters spent the 2020 season at the alternate site where he worked to improve his approach at the plate. He has added strength and has a solid work ethic and makeup. If he can carry over the refinements he made at the alternate site, he could be knocking on the door of the majors early in 2021. Waters might have even made the postseason roster if the Braves didn't already have Pache and his excellent glove on the depth chart.

Variance: High. The offensive potential is there and Waters has yet to be challenged in the minors. He may always be a high strikeout player due to the approach, but if the power develops he could be a star regardless.

Mark Barry's Fantasy Take: If you're a gambler, Waters can provide a sizable return on investment. There's a path to no-doubt fantasy stardom for the switch-hitter as a true five-category contributor. That's obviously hard to find. I'm a little worried about all of the swing-and-miss—Waters has incrementally been striking out at a higher clip since a 2018 stint in A-ball, culminating in a strikeout rate a tick above 36 percent in a small Triple-A sample. If he's going to strike out that much (and not walk very much) the batting average is going to dip and he'll have fewer opportunities for base thievery. Personally, I'd be a little more comfortable with Waters in that 20-25ish range as opposed to flirting with the top-10 for dynasty prospects.

★ ★ ★ *2021 Top 101 Prospect* **#62** ★ ★ ★

4 **Kyle Muller** LHP   OFP: 60 ETA: Late 2021
Born: 10/07/97 Age: 23 Bats: R Throws: L Height: 6'7" Weight: 250
Origin: Round 2, 2016 Draft (#44 overall)

The Report: Muller has come a long way since making his pro debut in 2016 with a fastball that sat in the upper-80s. He spent that offseason working at Driveline, and it has paid off as his velocity quickly jumped and has continued to rise.

That added velocity in 2019 did have a negative effect on Muller's command, however. Muller also throws a curveball and a changeup that can play above average when the command is there. Reports from the alternate site were that he showed improvement in his command but he will need to carry that into minor league games next season. He is a great athlete and can stick as a starter long term, but his stuff would also play well as a late-inning reliever.

Development Track: Muller was sitting in the upper 90s with quality spin and touched 100 with a potential plus changeup at the alternate site. He will be ticketed to begin the season at Gwinnett where the focus will again be on his command. There is no questioning the stuff, but he is going to have to show the ability to throw strikes and further refine the secondaries. Atlanta isn't going to rush him to the majors, but if he can show improvement with his strike throwing in Triple-A, a 2021 debut isn't out of the question.

Variance: High. Triple-digit velocity with one of the best fastball spin rates in the minors gets you to the majors, but the command issues could force him into a relief role.

Mark Barry's Fantasy Take: Muller flashing command improvements at the alternate site feels a little like my totally real, totally great middle school girlfriend who I met at camp who lives in Canada. Like, it would be incredible if it were real, but also the likelihood of that reality is unfortunately fairly slim. I think Muller is probably a reliever long term, and that's okay, as the Josh Haders and Dustin Mays have shown that there's still fantasy value in relief, even without saves.

───────── ★ ★ ★ *2021 Top 101 Prospect* **#81** ★ ★ ★ ─────────

5 **Shea Langeliers** C   OFP: 60   ETA: 2022
Born: 11/18/97   Age: 23   Bats: R   Throws: R   Height: 6'0"   Weight: 205
Origin: Round 1, 2019 Draft (#9 overall)

The Report: The Braves used the ninth pick in the 2019 draft on Langeliers and quickly sent him to Low-A for his professional debut. He was a little slow to come around at the plate but there was no questioning his defensive skills. Langeliers is a plus defender with a good arm, solid footwork, and plus pop times. He handles pitchers well and displays excellent leadership qualities.

Development Track: Offensively, Langeliers has elite raw power with a well-balanced swing from the right side, and he showed improved power to the opposite field at the alternate site. Langeliers is likely to start 2021 at High-A or Double-A, and while there are few questions about his defense, how his bat improves and whether or not he taps into his raw power with more consistency will determine how quickly he moves.

Variance: Medium. Langeliers' defensive tools are good enough that he won't need to hit a ton. There is enough power potential that, if the bat develops, it could push him to another level.

Mark Barry's Fantasy Take: "If the bat develops" dynasty catchers are one of my least favorite things, right up there with when someone quickly changes lanes right in front of you on the freeway, and then slows way down.

6. William Contreras   C   OFP: 55   ETA: Debuted in 2020
Born: 12/24/97   Age: 23   Bats: R   Throws: R   Height: 6'0"   Weight: 180
Origin: International Free Agent, 2015

The Report: Willson's younger brother has developed into a strong catching prospect himself, one quite distinct from his sibling in style. It's a bit of an all-or-nothing swing, meaning he will never have his older brother's batting average and on-base combo, but there's plus raw power waiting to be unleashed. He's made consistent strides behind the plate, and while he is athletic enough to perhaps have some positional flexibility, concerns he might have to move out from behind the plate have quieted down.

Development Track: Contreras broke summer camp with the Braves after both Tyler Flowers and Travis d'Arnaud were sidelined while in COVID-19 protocols. He was only up for the first few games, and tried to hit every fastball he saw—and some off-speed as well—to the moon. The swing is long even when he's not pressing, and he got beat consistently with velocity. He had 200 plate appearances above A-ball coming into 2020, so none of this is particularly concerning. He showed better hands behind the plate than expected which, combined with his plus arm and sound footwork, should make him an above-average overall catcher once the bat gets some more seasoning. It's not clear how much offensive upside is really in there, but .250 and 15 home runs is more than enough to start behind the plate, and he's got projection beyond that.

Variance: High. Contreras was overmatched by good fastballs too often in his major-league cameo. So the bat will need more seasoning in the minors, but the glove—especially receiving—has made enough strides that I think he will be back up sooner rather than later. While he's already been a major leaguer, the range of the ultimate outcomes is still pretty wide.

Mark Barry's Fantasy Take: Call me crazy (and absolutely DO NOT look at what I wrote last year), but I like Contreras more than Langeliers in a dynasty context. The bar at catcher is so low on offense that .250 with 15 homers and room for more is probably a back-end, mixed-league backstop, or a must-add in two-catcher leagues. It's not great, nor is it fun, but it's where we're at. Excitement!

7. Tucker Davidson   LHP   OFP: 50   ETA: Debuted in 2020
Born: 03/25/96   Age: 25   Bats: L   Throws: L   Height: 6'2"   Weight: 215
Origin: Round 19, 2016 Draft (#559 overall)

The Report: Davidson took a big step forward in 2019, upping his velocity while improving his secondary offerings. He added a slider to go along with an average curveball and a changeup. The curveball has good spin, but the slider may be the bigger weapon at this point. The fastball is low-to-mid-90s with improved command. Davidson had a solid spring, but was a little behind some of the other pitchers when summer camp opened, which delayed his debut until the final series of the regular season.

Development Track: Another good showing in spring training could put Davidson in contention for a rotation spot as soon as next season. He still needs to improve the slider and change to give him enough of an arsenal to be a starter, but if he's a reliever, he should be a good one.

Variance: Medium. There are enough durability concerns to see a relief role as the most likely outcome.

Mark Barry's Fantasy Take: Against my better judgment, I kinda/sorta like Davidson. The upside is iffy, but there's SP4-5 potential there which is definitely useful in 20-plus team leagues. That sounds like damning with faint praise, but I promise I don't mean it to be.

8. Braden Shewmake SS   OFP: 50   ETA: Late 2021
Born: 11/19/97   Age: 23   Bats: L   Throws: R   Height: 6'4"   Weight: 190
Origin: Round 1, 2019 Draft (#21 overall)

The Report: The Braves are famous for aggressively pushing their prospects with promotions and, in the span of six months, Shewmake went from the SEC to the Low-A Sally League to the Double-A Southern League. A big-framed shortstop—albeit on the lean side—he continued his hitting prowess that made him a first-round pick in 2019 out of Texas A&M. Even with a 6-foot-4 body, there is a significant question whether the power will ever manifest due to his swing mechanics, though the physicality is there to get the ball over the fence. The hands stay low and tend to lag behind, flattening out the bat-path and failing to provide a conducive launch angle. His contact rate is his calling card on offense, and with decent on-base numbers, it's more of a put-the-ball-in-play approach, keeping his strikeout numbers below average. Defensively, he is athletic and sure-handed enough to stick at short, with the belief he has the versatility to move around the diamond if asked.

Development Track: The advanced hit tool shown in 2019 would have likely landed him back in Mississippi for 2020, with clear areas to improve upon being strength gains and perhaps some swing tinkering without sacrificing too much contact. At Atlanta's alternate site there was talk of his natural power being put on display more regularly, which can only help the offensive-minded profile that features at least average-to-better defensive skills. The foundation of fundamentals could move him very quickly. However, with no clear path for playing time ahead of him in the majors, the Braves can slow-play Shewmake's development with no additional rush.

Variance: Medium. The thing about guys who hit for a lot of average and not much else is that they have to keep hitting for a lot of average to derive value.

Mark Barry's Fantasy Take: If you're not in a hurry, I like Shewmake as prospect depth. The Braves promoted him aggressively right out of the draft, and while he hasn't set the world ablaze, he has some big Chris Taylor/"Insert your favorite Rays utilityman here" vibes. With Dansby Swanson and Ozzie Albies in tow, they'll also be able to wait on moving Shewmake too quickly from here, which should help with his development. If you have a roster spot, there are worse ways to use it than waiting on Shewmake.

9

Jared Shuster   LHP   OFP: 50   ETA: 2023
Born: 08/03/98   Age: 22   Bats: L   Throws: L   Height: 6'3"   Weight: 210
Origin: Round 1, 2020 Draft (#25 overall)

The Report: A minor surprise as a first-round selection, Shuster benefited from his eye-popping numbers and performance during the abbreviated spring evaluation period. He was able to dominate with just two pitches, having arrived on campus with a plus changeup in his back pocket. His draft year ascent was dependent on adding to his fastball and improving his command. Both got upgrades following a strong campaign at the Cape Cod League. Shuster went from upper-80s on this heater to touching mid-90s with regularity. The arm action is very short, but that makes the release on his changeup deceptive, and that pitch has good downward fade. What is missing from the toolbox is a breaking ball up to par with his fastball and change. Presently, it's a below-average, slurvy offering he'll need to improve to be effective against both lefties and righties as a starter.

Development Track: As is usually the concern when a player takes a big leap from one year to the next, you want to see them replicate that success to ensure whatever changes made have subsequently stuck. With Shuster in particular, the emphasis will be on his delivery and the maturation of his breaking ball. The delivery is repeatable thanks to a very short arm action—which is good—but kinetically it leaves less room for further improvement on his velocity gains, which isn't as good. It also makes it harder to tinker with the breaking ball. He should be able to further its consistency to spot it for strikes, but it may never be a true swing-and-miss pitch.

Variance: High. The pressure put on the elbow with the kind of short arm action he has, while also needing to develop a snappier breaking ball, increases the risk profile. Shuster could inevitably end up being a very good reverse-split lefty with how good his changeup is against right-handed hitters.

Mark Barry's Fantasy Take: If Shuster figures out the breaking-ball-of-it-all, he's eminently more interesting. As it stands, I'm passing unless you're in a league that has 250ish prospects.

10

Michael Harris   OF   OFP: 55   ETA: 2023
Born: 03/07/01   Age: 20   Bats: L   Throws: L   Height: 6'0"   Weight: 195
Origin: Round 3, 2019 Draft (#98 overall)

The Report: The Braves went overslot in the third round to buy Harris out of a commitment to Texas Tech. He was a two-way player in high school, and a lot of teams preferred him on the mound. Atlanta liked him more as a hitter where he shows plus raw power as a switch-hitter with good bat-to-ball skills. He is a potential five-tool center fielder with a strong arm and plenty of upside.

Development Track: A return to Rome would seem to be in order for 2021 after Harris appeared in just 22 games in 2019. He spent time at the Braves' alternate training site this season.

Variance: Very High. Harris has all the tools and has been impressive during his short time as a professional. The swing can occasionally get long and he will need to refine his approach as he moves up through the system, but he is just at the beginning of his development. He struggled during his Low-A stint and needs to establish himself against more advanced pitching to jump past the safer names ahead of him.

Mark Barry's Fantasy Take: The top-shelf outcome is certainly exciting for Harris. The distance to the majors, however, keeps him on the watchlist for the next season, or so.

The Prospects You Meet Outside The Top Ten

MLB-ready, but probably relievers

Jasseel De La Cruz   RHP   Born: 06/26/97   Age: 24   Bats: R   Throws: R   Height: 6'1"   Weight: 195   Origin: International Free Agent, 2015

De La Cruz more or less held serve as the same fourth-starter/power-reliever prospect that charted at No. 10 on the Braves' list last offseason. He's closer to the majors now—even spending two separate days on the big-league roster as an unused bullpen arm—yet we're no closer to knowing the ultimate outcome. But we'll place a small bet on a setup guy with high-90s heat, a plus slider, and not quite good enough command to close.

Patrick Weigel   RHP   Born: 07/08/94   Age: 26   Bats: R   Throws: R   Height: 6'6"   Weight: 240   Origin: Round 7, 2015 Draft (#210 overall)

Weigel has bounced around a deep Braves system the past few list cycles; sometimes personal cheeseball, sometimes legit back-end starting prospect, occasionally out with Tommy John. He's settled in as a major-league-ready 95-and-a-slider guy. His mid-90s heater has a bit of run and he works it around the zone well. The slider doesn't always get ideal depth from his lower slot, but it's sharp even when it's sweepy. How the breaker ultimately plays will determine whether Weigel is more of a middle reliever or a setup man.

Prospects to dream on a little

Bryce Ball 1B Born: 07/08/98 Age: 22 Bats: L Throws: R Height: 6'6" Weight: 235 Origin: Round 24, 2019 Draft (#727 overall)
Ball was a 2019 post-draft darling as a 24th-rounder out of Dallas Baptist who immediately looked like he should've been popped in the first two rounds when unleashed in pro ball. He's a 70-power guy with a better feel for hitting than you'd think, although the overall projection is limited by a first base-only profile and swing-and-miss concerns. He was in consideration for the last couple of spots on this year's list, but ultimately we heard stronger things about how Harris developed at the alternate site than we did for Ball. We remain cautiously optimistic that he'll hit upper-level pitching, and disappointed that he didn't get that chance in 2020.

Mahki Backstrom 1B Born: 10/10/01 Age: 19 Bats: L Throws: L Height: 6'5" Weight: 220 Origin: Round 18, 2019 Draft (#547 overall)
Backstrom was taken six rounds earlier than Ball and signed away from Fresno State for a hair under $400,000. As a prep first baseman he's going to be a much slower burn than Ball, but the power upside here is significant—the swing isn't short, but the ball jumps like it's a slow pitch home run derby—and he only just turned 19.

You always need catching

Alex Jackson C Born: 12/25/95 Age: 25 Bats: R Throws: R Height: 6'2" Weight: 215 Origin: Round 1, 2014 Draft (#6 overall)
Jackson probably deserved a shot to become the league's latest power-and-defense hidden secret catcher after bopping 28 homers and grading out as the best defensive catcher in Triple-A in 2019. But Atlanta went out and signed Travis d'Arnaud, another former top prospect turned power-and-defense hidden secret. That one became less hidden when d'Arnaud ended up hitting .321 with power and his usual excellent framing; Jackson mostly remained stuck on the taxi squad. We continued to get positive feedback on his defense this season, a surprising turn given that he didn't catch until his fourth professional season.

Atlanta Braves 2021

Incumbent backup Tyler Flowers is a free agent and turns 35 in a couple months, so Jackson's shot could be coming in 2021, though Langeliers and especially Contreras are starting to look bigger in the rearview mirror.

Interesting draft follow

Spencer Strider   Born: 10/28/98   Age: 22   Bats: R   Throws: R   Height: 6'0"   Weight: 195   Origin: Round 4, 2020 Draft (#126 overall)

The Braves drafted Strider in the fourth round out of Clemson in 2020. He will need to prove himself after coming back from injury, but he offers a power arm with a chance to start. He was one of Atlanta's most impressive pitchers at fall instructs and touched 99 mph with a high-riding fastball. Strider also showed a plus curveball and is working to develop a changeup. The rotation is not out of the question, but he looks like he could be an impact arm out of the bullpen.

Top Talents 25 and Under (as of 4/1/2021):

1. Ronald Acuña Jr., OF
2. Ozzie Albies, 2B
3. Mike Soroka, RHP
4. Ian Anderson, RHP
5. Cristian Pache, OF
6. Austin Riley, 3B
7. Drew Waters, OF
8. Kyle Muller, LHP
9. Kyle Wright, RHP
10. Shea Langeliers, C

Ronald Acuña Jr. turns 23 in December and is one of the best baseball players in the universe. He was the first prospect we gave an 80 OFP to while I was on staff here at Baseball Prospectus. He's already lived up to it.

Ozzie Albies suffered through an injury-riddled 2020 season, hampered by a wrist injury. Yet going back to his major-league debut in 2017, he's never put up worse than a 106 DRC+, and he's a more-than-solid defender at second base. He was a four-plus win player in both 2018 and 2019, and the best could be yet to come if he puts it all together as he enters his mid-20s.

Soroka vs. Anderson was an extremely tough call. Soroka is only a year removed from being a Cy Young candidate, but he blew out his Achilles in his third start of 2020. In the end, he's just done it for longer than Anderson so far; if you want to go the other way because of the injury uncertainty or Anderson's more overpowering stuff, I certainly wouldn't begrudge you for it.

Austin Riley still hits the ball extremely hard and not enough. He made strides toward hitting it more in 2020, but his power dipped a little with the adjustments. The power potential here remains tantalizing if he can ever hit .270, and the whole package does play better at third base if he can stick at the hot corner. It's too many "if"s to rank higher in a loaded 25U list.

We've written what feels like books on Kyle Wright already. The short version is that he's perpetually one adjustment away from looking like a good major-league starter. The September 2020 flavor was repositioning him on the rubber; he ripped off four solid starts in a row down the stretch and in the NLDS and then completely imploded against the Dodgers in the NLCS. In his last year eligible for this list, I'm not sure we're truly any closer to figuring out whether he's going to get there than we were on the day he was drafted.

Part 3: Featured Articles

Braves All-Time Top 10 Players

by Matthew Trueblood

POSITION PLAYERS

JOE TORRE, C (1960–1968)
Big brother Frank Torre was a veteran first baseman for the Braves by the time Joe came up, which earned the rookie the benefit of the doubt. He never really needed it, though. In addition to being a solid backstop, the younger Torre hit .294/.356/.462 during his Braves tenure. He split his time between catching and playing first base after the first couple of seasons, but his bat could carry him even there. From 1964-66, he was a credible MVP candidate despite qualms about his mobility behind the plate.

FREDDIE FREEMAN, 1B (2010–Present)
For the last few years, there have been few purer, simpler joys than watching Freeman hit. His swing has a very short feel to it thanks largely to his two-handed finish and willingness to shoot the gap in left-center field. He makes pitchers work but is never looking to draw a walk: He swings at pitches within the zone at one of the highest rates in the league. Balletic (if not terribly rangy) at first base, he saves errors and occasionally steals outs for his team. As he's added more pull-field power to his arsenal, he's reached the MVP level he'd teased in the past, something validated by the BBWAA when they gave him the 2020 award.

EDDIE MATHEWS, 3B (1952–1966)
Mathews came along just in time to be a three-city Brave: He had one season in Boston, 13 in Milwaukee, and one in Atlanta. Along the way, he spent a decade as the best left-handed power hitter in the National League, whacking at least 40 home runs four times and at least 30 in nine straight seasons. He was patient at the plate, drawing 90-100 walks in most seasons. He didn't shine at third base, but he never needed to. He and Aaron were the cornerstones of the best teams in

Braves history. As good as Mathews was, he was held back by Milwaukee County Stadium; he had six seasons in which he averaged between .298 and .343 on the road, just one at home. Overall he hit .268/.375/.501 in Milwaukee as a Brave, .286/.395/.553 everywhere else. In 1953 he hit 17 home runs at home, but 30 on the road.

CHIPPER JONES, 3B/OF (1993–2012)

The consummate switch-hitter, Jones took full advantage of that ability. His plate discipline was extraordinary, leading to huge walk totals and low strikeout rates. He hit lefties and righties with almost perfectly equal skill and hit to all fields with power. A serious knee injury delayed his arrival by a year, but he was still a star as soon as he returned in 1995. From that season through 2008 he hit at least 20 home runs every year, despite being (if anything) a better hitter for average and doubles than for home-run power. At .303/.401/.529, he's the only player other than Rogers Hornsby to make the 3-4-5 club while playing an infield position other than first base.

JOHNNY LOGAN, SS (1951–1961)

Logan was a quintessential shortstop for his era, with more defense than offense although he had his share of the latter as well. Bridging the team's move from Boston to Milwaukee and a key role player as they pushed toward the front of the National League, he hit better than most middle infielders (though without much power and was below-average overall), ran the bases well, and was excellent in the field. From 1955-59, he was a four-time All-Star. From 1952-59, he was worth at least 2.0 WARP every year. A salty player, he was ejected 16 times, eight times for arguing balls and strikes, three times for fighting.

WALLY BERGER, OF (1930–1937)

Adjusting for an extreme pitcher's park and his era, Berger hit for monumental power, though he also struck out often. He was a power-hitting center fielder in an era that had very few of them, but his career was curtailed by multiple factors. He declined sharply after age 31, in 1937, and hurt his shoulder in 1940. The biggest push factor that drove him out of the game, though, might have been the greed of team owners. Berger was always unusually willing to fight for the salary he felt he deserved, and that led to friction between him and every team for which he played. Still, he was something of a miracle given Braves Field, which had huge dimensions and a cold wind that blew in off the Charles River. Berger hit 105 home runs there, more than twice as many as the runner up.

TOMMY HOLMES, OF (1942–1951)

We hear often about players whose careers were damaged or diminished by World War II. Holmes might be a player whose career was facilitated by it. A brilliant contact hitter, he played and hit for great averages in the Yankees chain for five years, but blocked by the historic Keller-DiMaggio-Henrich outfield he didn't get his shot in the big leagues until the war began and the ranks of available players began to thin. At that point he was helped by a second unusual factor, the longtime friendship between Yankees farm director George Weiss and Braves manager Casey Stengel, who made a you-scratch-my-back swap of something the Braves needed (a viable prospect of any kind) for something the Yankees needed (a veteran first baseman). Save for one season, 1945, he didn't hit for much power at all, but he hit a bonkers .352/.420/.577 that year. Among his other accomplishments that year were a National League-record 37-game hitting streak and a never-to-be-duplicated statistical oddity, leading the league in both home runs (28) and fewest strikeouts (9). For his career, he was a solid .302/.366/.432 hitter and a fine outfielder.

HENRY AARON, OF (1954–1974)

Early in his career, Aaron aspired not to Babe Ruth's records, but to Stan Musial's still-growing National League record for hits. It's reflected in the way he hit: he used to wait on a pitch away from him, then flick the ball forcefully with those famous wrists into the gap in right-center field. As he matured, he changed. He let those pitches go by, drew more walks, sat on offerings closer to him, pulled them, and his home run totals began to climb. He could make that kind of lane change, almost without sacrificing anything. He was that special. Once he went down that path, his calm temperament came into play; not every player could have withstood the intensifying attacks of threatened bigots, but he did. It's not a skill you can quantify on a baseball card, but it's real and as impressive as any of his others.

DALE MURPHY, OF (1976–1990)

Murphy was too big, too fast, and too good a hitter to be left at catcher, where it would have taken much longer to mill him into a big-leaguer. Freed from the confines of the catcher's box and allowed to roam center field, he blossomed immediately into one of the game's best power hitters. With a patient approach and a Ted Williams-inspired, top hand-dominant uppercut, he generated high on-base percentages, high strikeout rates, and gaudy home run totals throughout his prime. He was a viable center fielder in his 20s and a downright good right fielder in his 30s. Back-to-back MVPS in 1982 and 1983 (the latter a 30-30 season) testify to just how dominant he was at the time, something his relatively quick decline from 32 on helped to obscure.

ANDRUW JONES, OF (1996–2007)

According to Baseball-Reference's similarity scores, the player who Jones most resembled was Dale Murphy. What they have in common: Right-handed power and an early fall from their peak. What they don't have in common: Murphy, though he won five Gold Gloves, was not the generational defensive talent Jones was. His gliding, running form made Jones unusually good at tracking the ball in flight. It gave an odd (and sometimes off-putting) sense of effortlessness to his movements and led to unfair accusations that he didn't play hard, but he caught everything. Starting from impossibly shallow positions, he could make catches at the center-field wall. He routinely stole doubles with flying dives on line drives to the gaps. At the plate, he was unsubtle, but had the ability to barrel the ball up with regularity and grew into truly prodigious power as he grew out of his defensive wizardry).

PITCHERS

VIC WILLIS, RHP (1898–1905)

In 1902, Willis made 46 starts, and pitched 45 complete games. He also made five relief appearances. (Forget the stamina. Where did he find the time?) He pitched 410 innings, leading the major leagues. That kind of workload was his calling card, but he also had a handful of seasons as an ace-caliber pitcher on a per-batter basis. Relying on slow curves, he sometimes walked a lot of batters, but he was hard to square up.

DICK RUDOLPH, RHP (1913–1920, 1922, 1927)

The 1914 Miracle Braves, who came back from 15 games behind to win the pennant, could thank Rudolph for much of that outcome. From July 6 through the end of that season, he pitched in 24 games, starting 21 of them. He posted a 1.79 ERA in 201 innings, and the Braves went 21-3 when he appeared. One of the losses came on the final day of the season, long after they'd sealed the pennant, and Rudolph threw three scoreless innings even in that effort. He was a spitballer but faked loading the ball up at least as often as he actually did so. Hitters felt they had to be ready for that pitch and often ended up looking foolish on hittable fastballs. Not quite 5-foot-10, the Giants had first crack at him but failed to read his potential, and the Braves acquired him after he had several big seasons for Toronto.

JOHNNY SAIN, RHP (1942, 1946–1951)

Forced to wait until World War II was over to begin his career in earnest, just as Spahn was, Sain let out his pent-up enthusiasm by averaging 273 innings and posting a 3.37 ERA from 1946-50. Rex Barney, whose Dodgers faced Sain often during those years, said Sain could land a curveball in a coffee mug, and that praise was well-founded. Sain was a protomodern pitcher, throwing a steady diet of curves and fooling batters by hardly ever giving them a shot at his unimpressive fastball. After four 20-win seasons he was traded to the Yankees for Lew Burdette and $50,000, a deal the Braves got the better of as Sain had a moderate impact in a swingman/closer role while Burdette became a late-blooming All-Star.

WARREN SPAHN, LHP (1942, 1946–1964)
Seemingly refusing to have his career shortened after it was delayed by an early demotion and then service in the Second World War (unlike many ballplayers he saw combat and was wounded in the Battle of the Bulge), Spahn pitched into his mid-40s and remained above-average almost until the end. Randy Johnson is his only real rival for the title of greatest left-hander in history. Early in his career, Spahn threw a hard, rising fastball, and only needed a fairly standard-issue curveball and changeup to complement it. Later, after a knee injury compromised his power, he developed a circle-change that had screwball movement and kept him durable and dominant. Thus did he have consecutive 20-win seasons from his age-36 season through age-40, then added another (his 13th) at 42.

LEW BURDETTE, RHP (1951–1963)
The man from Nitro threw strikes and let the rest take care of itself. He sometimes gave up too many hits and homers to be excellent overall, but he was able to accumulate huge innings totals that way, and his refusal to issue free passes set a high floor for him—he walked just 1.8 batters per nine innings. The rule requiring a pitcher to step off the mound before going to their mouth traces to Burdette, whom opponents suspected of throwing spitters, sometimes even when he wasn't. His three complete-game wins (two of them shutouts) in the 1957 World Series made him the MVP of that series and a Milwaukee sports legend.

PHIL NIEKRO, RHP (1964–1983)
Most pitchers who feature the knuckleball bloom late because they only adopt the pitch as a last resort, as though the claw-like grip the pitch requires were not on the baseball but on a cliff face from which they were about to fall out of baseball. Niekro, though, learned the knuckleball from the time he was a small child… and still nearly fell off that cliff when the Braves came within a fingernail's width of releasing him in 1959. Like a latecomer to the knuckleball would, Niekro would be 26 before establishing himself in the majors. Once he mastered the pitch, though, he tortured hitters with it for almost a quarter-century. One of the few pitchers who withstood the insane workloads of the 1970s, and even thrived, although it put him in the odd position of having 20-win and 20-loss seasons.

TOM GLAVINE, LHP (1987–2002)
Thin and unimposing, Glavine was a better athlete than he appeared, having been a pro-caliber hockey player as well as a pitching prospect. Once he chose baseball, he embarked on a career of real craftsmanship, even if he sometimes benefited from friendly environs and the seeming ability to hypnotize umpires into giving him the benefit of the doubt on close pitches. Through 1993, 79.7

percent of his strikeouts came on swings and misses. Thereafter, that number plummeted to 62.6 percent, as umpires let Glavine establish wide corners and he took full advantage.

JOHN SMOLTZ, RHP (1988–2008)
For a stretch during his mid-20s, it seemed like Smoltz added a new pitch every year. At his best, he touched 98 miles per hour with his fastball, could switch to a turbo sinker, had one of the game's best sliders and its best splitter, and had two different changeups in which his confidence might vary from start to start. He pushed himself incredibly hard, to innings totals his arm (perhaps) shouldn't have borne and to return sooner from Tommy John surgery than he otherwise could have, even if it meant becoming a closer for a few years. His switch back to starting in his late 30s was only possible because he was such a great athlete and competitor.

GREG MADDUX, RHP (1993–2003)
The Yankees offered Maddux more money during the winter of 1992-1993, but the Braves' consecutive pennants and young core was a powerful pull factor. Maddux and Leo Mazzone could hardly have been better-suited to one another, in terms of pitching philosophy, and the rivalry of teammates between Maddux, Smoltz, Tom Glavine, and Steve Avery pushed all of them hard. His velocity had already declined to more-or-less average by the time he joined the Braves, but Maddux had gained the touch to cut, sink, and move the ball around the zone that would make him unhittable for years.

TIM HUDSON, SP (1999–2015)
Hudson tore his UCL in late July 2008, but made it back to help the Braves fight for the 2009 Wild Card. That might be the best one-sentence encapsulation of him, though that doesn't mean we can't say more. A beloved teammate, tough competitor, and excellent sinkerballer, Hudson kept the ball on the ground, piled up over 3,000 innings despite numerous injuries, and could be trusted in big moments. His ability to attack hitters with multiple changeups, working off a sinker, was fascinating.

A Taxonomy of 2020 Abnormalities

by Rob Mains

I'm going to start this with a trivia question. Trust me, it's relevant. Don't bother skipping to the end of the article to find the answer, it's not there.

Only five players have appeared in 140 or more games for 16 straight seasons. Who are they?

It's a trivia question starting off an essay, so you know how this works: Whatever you guessed, you're wrong. It's okay. As someone who purchased this book, chances are good that you're an educated baseball fan. But the circumstances behind 2020 force us to abandon, or at least seriously question, some of our favorite patterns and crutches for evaluating the game we love.

We just completed what was undoubtedly the strangest season in MLB history. No fans, geographically limited schedule, universal DH, seven-inning twin bills, runners on second in extra innings, a 16-team postseason, a club playing at a Triple-A stadium. Some of these changes will likely persist (sorry), but we've never had so many tweaks dumped on us all at once, at least not since they figured out how many balls were in a walk.

And the biggest, of course, was the 60-game season. The 19th century was dotted with teams that went bankrupt before the season ended, but the lone season with only 60 scheduled games was 1877. That year there were only six teams, the league rostered a total of 77 players (just 16 more than the 2020 Marlins), and batters called for pitches to be thrown high or low by the pitcher, who was 50 feet away. We can say the 2020 season was easily the shortest ever for recognizable baseball.

As such, it'll stand out. Few abbreviated seasons do. Just about everybody reading this knows the 1994 season ended after Seattle's Randy Johnson struck out Oakland's Ernie Young for the last out of the Mariners-A's game on August 11. The ensuing player strike wiped out the rest of the season and the postseason. Teams played only 112-117 games that year.

And many of you know that a strike in the middle of the 1981 season split the season in two, resulting in the only Division Series until 1995. Teams played only 103-111 games that year, the shortest regular season since 1885.

Those two seasons are memorable. So when we see that nobody drove in 100 runs in 1981, or that Greg Maddux was the only pitcher with 180 or more innings pitched in 1994, we think, "Of course. Strike year."

But we don't remember other short years. You might not recall that the 1994 strike spilled into the next year, chopping 18 games off the 1995 schedule. You might've read that the 1918 season, played during the last pandemic, ended after Labor Day due to the government's World War I "work or fight" order. A strike erased the first week and a half of the 1972 season, but that year's best known as the last time pitchers batted in the American League.

The point is, while we don't remember small changes to the schedule, we remember the big ones. The 1981 mid-season strike. The 1994 season- and Series-ending strike. And, of course, the pandemic-shortened 2020 season. We won't need a reminder why Marcell Ozuna's 18 homers were the fewest to lead the National League in a century. (Literally; Cy Williams led with 15 in 1920.)

Now, about that trivia question. The five players are Hank Aaron, Brooks Robinson, Pete Rose, Ichiro Suzuki, and Johnny Damon. The one nobody gets, of course, is Damon, and a lot of people miss Ichiro, whose last season of 140-plus games came garbed in the red-orange and ocean blue of Miami when he was 42. That's half of what makes it a good question. The other half is the two guys whom many think made the list but didn't. Lou Gehrig? His streak started in the Yankees' 42nd game of the 1925 season and lasted only 13 seasons after that. And everybody assumes Cal Ripken Jr. did it, having played 2,632 straight games over 17 seasons. But one of those 17 seasons was 1994, when the Orioles played only 112 games.

My point? *I just told you* everybody remembers the 1994 strike year, but everybody forgets it fell in the middle of Ripken's streak, separating the first twelve years from the last four. Just because we recall something doesn't mean it's always at the front of our minds.

Nobody is going to forget 2020, and baseball is obviously not the main reason. But there will come a time in the future when you're looking at a player's or a team's record, and there will be baffling numbers there for 2020, and you'll think, "I wonder what happened." (Not to mention the missing line for minor league players.) Just like you forgot that the 1994 strike limited Ripken to 112 games.

Try not to forget it, though. The 2020 season resulted in weird statistical results for several reasons.

There were only 60 games.
I know, duh. But that had impacts beyond counting stats like Ozuna's home run total or Yu Darvish and Shane Bieber leading the majors with eight wins. (I know, pitcher wins, but still.)

The 162-game season is the longest among major North American sports, and that duration gives us a gift. Over the course of a long season, small variations tend to even out. A player who has a ten-game hot streak will probably have a ten-game cold streak. A team that starts the year losing a bunch of close games will probably win a bunch of them. We get regression to the mean. Statistics stabilize.

Consider flipping a coin. Over the long run, we expect it to come up heads about half the time. But the fewer flips, the more variation there'll be. If you flip a coin six times, probability theory tells us you'll get at least two-third heads about 34 percent of the time. Flip it 30 times, your chance of two-thirds heads drops to five percent.

Or, relevant to this case, if you flip a coin 60 times, your chance of getting at least 36 heads—that's 60 percent—is 7.75 percent. Expand the coin-flipping to 162 times, and the chance of getting 60 percent heads drops to 0.73 percent.

In other words, the odds of an outcome that's 20 percent better (or worse) than expected is *more than ten times higher* when you flip your coin 60 times than when you do it 162 times. Call it small sample size, call lack of mean reversion, or call it luck not evening out, 162 is a lot more predictive than 60. You get much more variation over 60 games than over 162. Bieber's 1.63 ERA and 0.87 FIP aren't something we'd see over a full season, and neither is Javier Baéz's .203/.238/.360.

Some players' lines in 2020 look normal. Brian Anderson had an .811 OPS in 2019 and an .810 OPS in 2020. (He probably would have gotten that last point if he'd been given enough time.) But there are many like Bieber and Baéz, some of them from young players still establishing their talent levels. The answer to the question, "What went right or wrong for that guy in 2020?" is most likely "Nothing, it was just a 2020 thing."

Preseason training was abbreviated for hitters.

Every year, spring training drags. Players get tired of it, fans get tired of it, and you sure can tell sportswriters get tired of it. Yes, something to get everyone into shape is necessary, but does it really have to drag on for over a month? Can't we shorten it?

The 2020 season answered in the negative, at least for hitters. Warren Spahn is credited with saying that hitting is timing and pitching is upsetting timing. It appears nobody had his timing down after the abbreviated July summer camp. Through August 9—18 games into the season—MLB batters were hitting .230/.311/.395 with a .275 BABIP. That BABIP, had it held, would have been the lowest since 1968, the Year of the Pitcher. In recent years it's hovered around .300.

It didn't hold. Play returned to more normal levels the rest of the year: .249/.325/.425 with a .297 BABIP starting August 10. But batters whose play concentrated in those first two weeks wound up with ugly lines. Andrew

Benintendi went on the injured list with a season-ending rib cage strain on August 11. His final line: .103/.314/.128 in 14 games. Franchy Cordero went on the IL with a hamate bone fracture on August 9 and a .154/.185/.231 line. Even though he came back strong in a late September return, it was too late to repair his full-season numbers.

Preseason training was abbreviated for pitchers.

Every year, spring training drags. Players get tired of it, fans get tired of it … wait, I already said that. But the abbreviated preseason was tough on pitchers, too. As noted, they had the upper hand coming out of the gate. But then they lost that hand. And then their arms, too.

The 2020 season was spread over 67 days. During those 67 days, 237 pitchers hit the Injured List, compared to 135 in the first 67 days of 2019. A lot of those IL stints, though, were COVID-19-related. Still, over the first 67 days of the 2019 season, there were 72 pitchers on the IL with arm injuries. That figure jumped to 110 in 2020, a 53 percent increase.

There are a number of factors contributing to pitcher arm injuries, ranging from usage to velocity, but it appears that attenuated preseason training played a role. A lot of pitchers had super-short seasons due to arm woes. Corey Kluber, Roberto Osuna, and Shohei Ohtani combined for seven innings, none after August 8. All suffered arm injuries. We'll never know whether they'd have fared better with a longer preseason, but we can guess how they probably feel.

Everybody played.

Rosters were set to expand from 25 to 26 in 2020, so even if we'd had a normal season, we'd have likely seen 2019's record of 1,410 players on MLB rosters broken. But due to the pandemic, rosters started the year at 30 and were cut to only 28. Add multiple COVID-19 absences and the revolving door caused by poor starts by hitters and a rash of pitcher arm injuries, and 1,289 players appeared in MLB games in 2020. The comparable figure over the first 67 days of the 2019 season was 1,109. That 16 percent increase works out to an average of six more players per team in 2020 compared to a similar slice of 2019. A future look back at 2020 rosters will include a lot of unfamiliar names.

Plus became a minus.

In advanced metrics, we adjust batter and pitcher performance for park and league/era variations. A plus sign appended to the end of a measure means that it's adjusted for park and league. It's scaled to an average of 100, with higher figures above average and lower figures below average. (Similarly, a metric with a minus is also park- and league-adjusted and scaled to 100, with lower values better.) Here at BP, our advanced measure of offensive performance is DRC+. Baseball-Reference has OPS+ and FanGraphs has wRC+.

Using park and league adjustments, we can compare Dante Bichette's 1995 Steroid Era season at pre-humidor Coors Field (.340/.364/.620, 40 homers, 128 RBI, MVP runner-up) with Jim Wynn's 1968 Year of the Pitcher season at the cavernous Astrodome (.269/.376/.474, 26 homers, 67 RBI, no MVP votes). It's not close. DRC+, OPS+, and wRC+ all give the nod to Wynn, handily. This is a useful tool. As my Baseball Prospectus colleague Patrick Dubuque tweeted last fall, "Please note that when I ask how you are, I am already adjusting for era."

The 2020 season messes up plus (and minus) stats for two reasons. First, the park adjustment was based on only 30 home games instead of the usual 81. Everything noted above regarding the short season applies, literally doubly, to park effect calculations. DRC+ uses a single-season park factor. OPS+ uses a three-year average and wRC+ five years. The figure for 2020 is suspect.

Second, OPS+ and wRC+ adjust for league: American and National. (DRC+ adjusts for opponent, regardless of league.) While there were two leagues in 2020, they were an artificial construct. To reduce travel, teams played opponents geographically, not based on league. There weren't two leagues, American and National. There were three, Western, Central, and Eastern.

That makes a difference because teams in the same league played in different run-scoring environments. AL teams scored 4.58 runs per game, NL teams 4.71. That's a small difference. But teams in the East scored 0.21 more runs per game (4.95) than teams in the West (4.74), and they both scored a lot more than Central teams (4.25). Adjusting for league misses that difference, so this book will be safe in that regard, but other sources may be distorted somewhat.

Not every game was a "game."

In 2020, the rising tide of strikeouts was finally stemmed. Strikeouts per team per game fell from 8.8 in 2019 to 8.7 in 2020. That marked the first decline after 14 straight annual increases.

In 2020, the rising tide of strikeouts rose higher. Batters struck out in 23.4 percent of plate appearances compared to 23.0 percent in 2019. That marked the 15th straight annual increase.

Both are true statements.

Because of two rule changes—seven-inning doubleheaders and runners on second in extra innings—games in 2020 were unprecedented in their brevity. There were 37.0 plate appearances per game in 2020. The only years with fewer were 1904 and 1906-1909. The average game in 2020 entailed 8.61 innings pitched, the fewest since 1899.

So when you see any per-game stats for 2020, you need to increase them by 3 or 4 percent to get them on equal footing with recent years.

Atlanta Braves 2021

Or, better, just ignore them. Last year happened. There were major league games contested between major league teams. But when you're looking at those physical or electronic baseball cards, when you're weaving narratives over why this young player's inevitable rise to stardom fell apart or why that old veteran rekindled his magic, don't linger on the 2020 line. It was just too weird.

Thanks to Lucas Apostoleris for research assistance.

—*Rob Mains is an author of Baseball Prospectus.*

Tranches of WAR

by Russell A. Carleton

We ask "replacement level" to be a lot of things. Sometimes contradictory things. Sometimes I wonder if we know what it even means anymore. The original idea was that it represented the level of production that a team could expect to get from "freely available talent", including bench players, minor leaguers, and waiver wire pickups. It created a common benchmark to compare everyone to, and for that reason, it represented an advancement well beyond what was available at the time. In fact, it created a language and a framework for evaluating players that was not just better but *entirely* different than what came before it.

But then we started mumbling in that language. The idea behind "wins above replacement" was one part sci-fi episode and one part mathematical exercise. Imagine that a player had disappeared before the season and suddenly, in an alternate timeline, his team would have had to replace him. The distance between him and that replacement line was his value. We need to talk about that alternate timeline.

Without getting too into 2:00 am "deep conversations" with extensive navel-gazing, it's worth thinking about why one player might not be playing, while another might.

- A player might not be playing because he has a short-term injury or his manager believes that he needs a day off.
- A player might not be playing because he has a longer-term injury that requires him to be on the injured list.

There's a difference here between these two situations. In particular, the first one generally *doesn't* involve a compensatory roster move, while the second one does. It's possible, though not guaranteed, that the person who will be replacing the injured/resting player would be the same in either case. That matters. Teams generally carry a spare part for all eight position players on the diamond, although in the era of a four-player bench, those spare parts usually are the backup plan for more than one spot.

A couple of years ago, I posed a hypothetical question. Suppose that a team had two players in its system fighting for a fourth outfielder spot. One of them was a league average hitter, but would be worth 20 runs below average if allowed to play center field for a full season. One of them was a perfectly average fielder, but would be 15 runs below average as a hitter, if allowed to play an entire season. Which of the two should the team roster? It's tempting to say the second one, as overall, he is the better player. That misses the point. A league average hitter on the bench isn't just a potential replacement for an injured outfielder. He might also pinch hit for the light-hitting shortstop in a key spot. You keep the average hitter on the roster, even though he isn't a hand-in-glove fit for one specific place on the field, because being a bench player is a different job description than being a long-term fill-in for someone. If you find yourself in need of a longer-term fill-in, you can bring the other guy up from AAA.

When we're determining the value of an everyday player though, if he had disappeared before the season and a team would have had to replace his production, they likely would have done it with a player who was a long-term fill-in type because they would have had to replace a guy who played everyday. Maybe that's the same guy that they would have rostered on their bench anyway, but we don't know. It gets to the query of what we hope to accomplish with WAR. Are we looking for an accurate modeling of reality or are we looking for a common baseline to compare everyone to? Both have their uses, but they are somewhat different questions.

Let's talk about another dichotomy.

- A player might not be playing because he isn't very good and is a bench-level player.
- A player might not be playing because there is another player on the team who has a situational advantage that makes him the better choice today. The classic case of this is a handedness platoon. On another day, he might be a better choice.

When we think about player usage, I think we're still stuck in the model that there are starters and there are scrubs. We have plenty of words for bench players or reserves or backups or utility guys. We do still have the word "platoon" in our collective vocabulary, but in the age of short benches, it's hard to construct one. It's always been hard to construct them. You have to find two players who hit with different hands, have skill sets that complement each other, and probably play the same position. In the era of the short bench, one of them had probably better double as a utility player in some way. Baseball has a two-tiered language geared toward the idea of regulars and reserves. The fact that it was so easy for me to find plenty of synonyms for "a player whose primary function is to come into a game to replace a regular player if he is injured or resting" should tell you something.

I'm always one to look for "unspoken words" in baseball. What is it called when someone is both half of a platoon and the utility infielder? That guy exists sometimes, but he reveals himself in that role—usually by accident. We don't have a word for that, and whenever I find myself saying "we don't have a word for that", I look for new opportunities. What do you call it, further, when the job of being the utility infielder is decentralized across the whole infield with occasional contributions from the left fielder? It's not even a "super-utility" player. What happens when you build your entire roster around the idea that everyone will be expected to be a triple major?

⚾   ⚾   ⚾

I think someone else beat me to this one, and on a grand scale. Platoons work because we know that hitters of the opposite hand to the pitcher get better results than hitters of the same hand, usually to the tune of about 20 points of OBP. If you want to express that in runs, it usually comes out to somewhere around 10 to 12 runs of linear weights value prorated across 650 PA. But hang on a second, now let's say that we have two players who might start today, both of roughly equal merit with the bat. One has a handedness advantage, but is the worse fielder of the two. In that case, as long as his "over the course of a season" projection as a fielder at whatever position you want to slot him into is less than a 10-run drop from the guy he might replace, then he's a better option today.

We're not used to thinking of utility players as bat-first options, who would play below-average defense at three different infield positions. That guy might hook on as a 2B/3B/LF type (Howie Kendrick, come on down!) but teams usually think to themselves that they need as their utility infielder someone who "can handle" shortstop, the toughest of the infield spots to play. If someone can do that *and* hit well, he's probably already starting somewhere, so he's not available as a utility infielder. It's easier for those glove guys to find a job. In a world where the replacement for a shortstop *has to be* the designated utility infielder, that makes sense.

But as we talked about last week, we're living in a different world. The rate at which a replacement for a regular starter turns out to be *another starter* shifting over to cover has gone way up over the last five years. There was always some of it in the game, but this has been a supernova of switcheroos. Now if your second baseman is capable of playing a decent shortstop, that 2B/3B/LF guy can swap in. He's not actually playing shortstop, and maybe the defense suffers from the switch, but if he's got enough of a bat, he might outhit those extra fielding miscues. And in doing so, he is effectively your backup shortstop.

Somewhere along the lines, teams got hip to the idea of multi-positional play from their regulars. I've written before about how you can't just put a player, however athletic, into a new position and expect much at first. The data tell us that. Eventually, players can learn to be multi-positionalists, but it takes time, roughly on the order of two months, before they're OK. But there's a hidden message in there. If you give a player some reps at a new spot, he's a reasonably gifted athlete and somewhat smart and willing to learn, he could probably pick it up enough to get to "good enough," and it doesn't take forever. You just have to be purposeful about it. Maybe you get to the point where you can start to say "he's still below average but we could move him there and get another bat into the lineup, and it's a net win."

Teams have started to build those extra lessons into their player development program. It used to be seen as a mark of weakness to be relegated to "utility player" because that meant that you were a bench player (all those synonyms above come with a side of stigma). Now, it's a way of building a team. If you get a few reps in the minors (where it doesn't count) at a spot, you'll have at least played the spot at game speed before. There are limits to how far you can push that. A slow-footed "he's out in left field because we don't have the DH" guy is never going to play short, but maybe your third baseman can try second base and not look like a total moose out there.

⚾ ⚾ ⚾

Back to WAR. I'd argue that the world of starters and scrubs is slowly disintegrating, for good cause. In the event that a regular starter really does go down with an injury–ostensibly, the alternate universe scenario that WAR is attempting to model–it makes the team a little more resilient to replacing him. And the good news is that you're more likely to be able to replace him with the best of the bench bunch, rather than the third-best guy, because the best guy doesn't have to be an exact positional match for the guy who got hurt. And that's what the manager would want to do. He'd want to replace that long-term production, not with an amalgam of everyone else who played that position, but with the best guy available from his reserves.

Now this is still WAR. We still want to retain the principle that we should be measuring a player, and not his teammates. We need some sort of common baseline, and despite what I just said, we'll still need some sort of amalgam. To construct that, I give to you the idea of the tranche. The word, if you've not heard it before, refers to a piece of a whole that is somehow segmented off. It's often used in finance to talk about layers of a financial instrument.

Here, I want you to consider that there are 30 starters at each of the seven non-battery positions (catchers should have their own WAR, since only a catcher can replace a catcher). We can identify them by playing time, and we can futz around with the definition a little bit if we need to. Next, among those who aren't in that starting pool, we identify the top tranche of the 30 best bench players, which I would again identify by playing time, and then the second and third and fourth and so on. If a player were to disappear, his manager would probably want to take a guy from that top tranche of the bench to replace him. In a world where even the starters can slide around the field, that becomes more feasible.

We can take a look at that top tranche and say "How many of them showed that they are able to play (first, second, etc.)?" and therefore could have directly substituted for the starter? How many of them could have been a direct substitute for our injured player? We don't know whether one of them would be on *a specific* team, but we can say that 40 percent of the time, a manager would have been able to draw from tranche 1 in filling the role, and 35 percent from tranche 2. But on tranche 1, we can also look at how many of those players played a position that could have then shifted and covered for that spot. We'd need some eligibility criteria for all of this (probably a minimum number of games played) but it would just be a matter of multiplication. Shortstop would be harder to fill, and managers would probably be dipping a little further down in the talent pool, and so replacement level would be lower, as it is now.

Doing some quick analysis, I found that the difference in just batting linear weights (haven't even gotten into running or fielding) between tranche 1 and tranche 2 in 2019 was about 6.5 runs, prorated across 650 PA. Between tranche 1 and tranche 3, it's 10.8 runs. The ability to shift those plate appearances up the ladder has some real value.

This part is important. We can also give credit to starters for the positions that they showed an ability to play, even if they didn't play them (this is the guy fully capable of playing center, but who's in a corner because the team already has a good center fielder) because he allows a team to carry a player who hits like a left fielder to functionally be the team's backup center fielder. He facilitates that movement upward among the tranches. We can start to appreciate the difference between a left fielder who would never be able to hack it in center (and the compensatory move that his team would have to make) and the left fielder who could do it, but just didn't have to very often.

Past that, you can continue to use whatever hitting and fielding and running metrics you like to determine a player's value, but when we get down to constructing that baseline, I'd argue we need a better conceptual and mathematical framework. It's going to require some more #GoryMath than we're used to, but I'd argue it's a better conceptualization of the way that MLB actually plays the game in 2020. If...y'know...MLB plays in 2020. If WAR is going to be our flagship statistic among the *acronymati*, then we need to acknowledge that it contains some old and starting-to-be-out-of-date assumptions about the game. We may need to tinker with it. Here's my idea for how.

—*Russell A. Carleton is an author of Baseball Prospectus.*

Secondhand Sport

by Patrick Dubuque

Back before time stopped, I liked to go to thrift stores. Now that I'm older, I rarely ever buy anything—I don't need much in my life, now—but I still enjoy the old familiar circuit: check to see if there are baseball cards to write about, look for board or card games to play with the kids, scan for random ironic jerseys, hit the book section. It takes ten, maybe fifteen minutes. Thrift stores are the antithesis of modern online shopping, because you don't know what they have, and you don't even really know what you want. It's junk, literal junk, stuff other people thought was worthless. That's what makes it great.

In an idealized economy, thrift stores shouldn't exist. Everybody has a living wage, and every product has a durability that exactly matches its desired life; nothing should need to be given away, no one should need to be given to. But then, thrift stores shouldn't work on a customer experience level, either. You wouldn't think an ethos of "let's make everything disorganized and hard to find" would lead to customer satisfaction, but low-budget retailers like TJ Maxx and Ross thrive on this model. People like bargain hunting as much for the hunting as the bargain; it's part of the experience, spending time as if it's a wager. There's a thrill, occasionally, in inefficiency.

In sports, the modern overuse of the word "inefficiency" is a condemnation: It insinuates that there is *an* efficiency, a correct way to be found, and that all other ways are wrong ways. It's prevalent in baseball but hardly contained to it; the lifehack, the Silicon Valley disruption are other examples of productivity creep in our daily lives. Their modern success makes plenty of sense. Maximization of resources, after all, is its own puzzle, and an industry of European board games is founded upon it. It's fun to take a system and optimize it, unravel it like a sudoku puzzle. If there's only one kind of genius, after all, there's no way anyone can fail to appreciate it.

Baseball has been hacking away at these perceived inefficiencies since its inception: platoons, bullpens, farm systems were all installed to extract more out of the tools at hand. But it's been a particular badge of the sabermetric movement, from Ken Phelps and his All-Star Team to Ricardo Rincon and the darlings of *Moneyball*. It's business, but it's also an ethos: the idea that there's treasure among the trash, something we all failed to appreciate until someone brought it to light.

It's the myth that made Sidd Finch so enticing, that fuels so many "best shape" narratives and new pitch promises. We all, athletes and unathletic sportswriters, want to believe that there's genius trapped inside us, and that it's just a matter of puzzling out the combination to unlock it. That our art, our style is the next inefficiency, waiting for our own Billy Beane. It's why we root for underdogs, and why we're excited for the Mike Tauchmans and the Eurubiel Durazos, champions of skin-deep mediocrity.

Except we aren't anymore, really. The days of "Free X" have descended beyond the ring of irony and into obscurity. There are still Xs to be freed, or at least one X, duplicated endlessly: Mike Ford, Luke Voit, Max Muncy. The undervalued one-dimensional slugger demonstrated how the game hasn't quite culturally caught up to its logical extreme. But for those who don't fit the rather spacious mold, times are grimmer. As Rob Arthur revealed several months ago, there's been a marked increase in the number of sub-replacement relievers. It's the outcome of a greater number of teams forced to play out games without the talent to win them, but it's also emblematic of the modern tendency of teams to dispose of their disposable assets, burning through cost-controlled arms the way that man chopped down forests in *The Lorax*. Stuff just isn't built to outlive their original owners anymore.

It's unsurprising, given how well-mined the market for inefficiencies has been of late. The disciples of the early analytics departments, and the disciples of those, have proliferated the league, with only a few backwater holdouts. The league has grown smarter, but every team has learned the same lesson. In fact, the phenomenon creates a peculiar kind of feedback loop: As teams value a specific subset of players or skills, prospective athletes learn to increase their own marketability by conforming themselves to the demands of their prospective employers.

And that's tragic, in the way that the extinction of animals is tragic; a certain amount of biodiversity in baseball has been lost. Shortstops hit like outfielders. Pitchers don't hit at all. Only the catchers remain idiosyncratic, thanks to the defensive demands of their position; eventually they too will be required to produce like everyone else, or they'll meet the fate of their battery mates. A perfect economy requires perfect production.

I mentioned earlier that more and more, I leave thrift stores empty-handed. It is true that I am more discerning than in the past; my bookshelves are full, and there are more streaming films than I will ever be able to watch. But there are other factors at play.

Thrift stores are, in a way, the bond markets of retail. When the economy is rough and other retailers are struggling, more people look secondhand for their products. But as recently as last year, publications were noting a reversal of the trend: Companies like Goodwill and Savers were expanding despite a strong economy. Publications credited a heightened sense of environmentalism and a rejection of cutting-edge fashion as drivers behind the increase, though the more likely answer is the modern American economy hasn't showered its favors equally, particularly among the young.

But it is more than just the economy. Baseball and thrift stores share something else in common, evident in our current conversations about re-starting the sport: They live in the gray area between public service and private enterprise. Thrift stores provide affordable necessities to lower-class citizens, and collectibles and fashion for the middle-class. Because of the success of the latter, prices have gone up across the board. Especially in terms of clothing, the middle-class flight from fashion into vintage has instead carried the aftereffects of fashion, including its costs, into a territory where people just want clothes. But there's another factor in the rise of prices, in the form of the internet.

The Goodwills of the world have grown smarter, too, employing the internet to extract full value from their detritus. Ebay, similarly, has lost much of the charm it had as a new frontier around the turn of the century. Everything has a price point now; even individual taste is no match for the algorithm, because anything rare, no matter how niche its market, is a collectible to someone.

The internet has had the same effect on thrift stores that sabermetrics has had on baseball; its equivalent to OBP was the bar scanner. As detailed in Slate, the rise of second-party stores on eBay and Amazon birthed an entire industry of used-good salespeople, armed with PDAs and scanners, buying books for three dollars to sell online for five. The author, Michael Savitz, reports earning $60,000 by working nearly 80 hours a week; he makes it clear that this is not a vocation of his choosing. It's long hours, with no real creativity or individuality, skimming the cream off of a local establishment and flipping it to someone with a little more money on the other side of the country. And once the vocation exists, the obvious question arises: why wait to put the wares out on the shelves? Why allow value to exist at all?

Nothing is ruined. Thrift stores will continue to sell polo shirts and DVDs, and baseball will continue to exist and make or lose money, depending on who you believe. But as we continue to refine our knowledge, we lose something in the conquest for efficiency, a delight born out of the unknown. The problem isn't the efficiency itself; we can't blame the booksellers, or the people sweeping freeways to collect grams of platinum from damaged catalytic converters. The problem is a system that requires this sort of profit-skimming behavior in order to feed families (or, for corporations, maximize shareholder return).

Atlanta Braves 2021

In times like these, with the 2020 season on the brink and the collective bargaining agreement close behind, it can often feel like the current situation is untenable. It can't keep going like this, even if we don't know what to do about it. But as with thrift stores, there's an equally irresistible feeling that it *has* to keep going, that it would be unimaginable to not have this broken, amazing sport. Both industries exist on an invisible foundation of friction, of chaos and unpredictability, even as both see their foundations buffed down to a perfect, untouchable polish. But if COVID-19 and its financial ramifications do, as some have suggested, make it such that the baseball that returns is fundamentally different than the baseball that came before, perhaps this is the time to lean in, and change the game even more. Fix bunting. Make defense more difficult. Create viable, alternate strategies. Add some chaos back into baseball. It's fun when no one knows quite where things are.

—Patrick Dubuque is an author of Baseball Prospectus.

Steve Dalkowski Dreaming

by Steven Goldman

We dream of being a pitcher, of starring in the major leagues. Depending on your age and your sense of historical perspective, you might imagine yourself as Walter Johnson, throwing harder than anyone else—hitting more batters than anyone else, too, but always feeling bad about it. You could picture yourself as a Tom Seaver or a David Cone, with all the stuff in the world but still being cerebral about it, thinking about so much more than burning 'em in there. There are so many models one could choose: You could be a Lefty Gomez, Jim Bouton, or Bill Lee, skilled, but not taking the whole thing too seriously, or a Lefty Grove, Bob Gibson, or Steve Carlton, powerful but treating each start like a mission to be survived instead of a game to be enjoyed.

Very few would dream of being Steve Dalkowski, the former Baltimore Orioles prospect who died of COVID-19 last week at the age of 80. Yet, there is something just as noble in Dalkowski's negative accomplishments—and accomplishments is what they are—as there is in the precision-engineered pitching of a Greg Maddux. You have to be very good to be that bad. Dalkowski had all of the stuff of the greatest pitchers but none of the command; his story is not one of failing to conquer his limitations, but striving against one of the cruelest hands that fate or genetics or personality can deal us: A desire to achieve great things which is almost but not quite matched by the ability to meet that goal.

As with Johnson, Grove, Bob Feller, and the rest of the hard-throwing pitchers who played before the advent of modern radar guns, we have to take the word of the players and coaches who saw Dalkowski pitch as to his velocity. He was a hard-drinking, maximum-effort pitcher who, if their memories are to be believed, consistently threw over 100 miles per hour. His was the Maltese Fastball, the stuff that dreams are made of. The problem is that velocity without command and control is still a good distance from utility. Dalkowski was the most effective towel you could design for a fish, the sleekest bathing suit intended to be worn by an astronaut, but that doesn't mean he wasn't beautiful: We can appreciate a journey even if it doesn't end at the intended destination.

Whether because of sloppy mechanics he couldn't calm, an inability to understand that a consistent 98 in the strike zone would likely be more effective than a consistent 110 out of it, or all that beer, Dalkowski could never make the adjustments that pitchers like Feller and Nolan Ryan made before him, possibly because he had so far to go: Feller, who never pitched in the minors, came up at 17 and spent three years walking almost seven batters per nine innings before settling in at 3.8 beginning when he was 20. Ryan started out walking over six batters per nine but gradually improved as his long career played out; for him to go from 6.2 walks per nine with the 1966 Greenville Mets to 3.7 with the 1989 Texas Rangers represents a 40 percent reduction. An equivalent improvement by Dalkowski would still have left him walking over 11 batters per nine innings.

Dalkowski was like *The Room* of pitchers, a player so bad he became good again. Cal Ripken, Sr., who both played with and managed Dalkowski, recalled in a 1979 *Sporting News* "where are they now" piece the occasion when the pitcher crossed up his catcher and his fastball, "hit the plate umpire smack in the mask. The mask broke all to pieces and the umpire wound up in the hospital for three days with a concussion. If they ever had a radar gun in those days, I'll bet Dalkowski would have been timed at 110 miles an hour."

Signed by the Orioles out of New Britain High in Connecticut in 1957, Dalkowski was sent to Kingsport in the Appalachian League, where he pitched 62 innings. He allowed only 22 hits in 62 innings, or 3.2 per nine, a number with no equivalent in major league history (though Aroldis Chapman came close in 2014), and also struck out 121 (17.6 per nine) and walked 129 (18.7). He was also charged with 39 wild pitches. That June, one of his fastballs clipped a Dodgers prospect named Bob Beavers and carried away part of his ear. "The first pitch was over the backstop, the second pitch was called a strike, I didn't think it was," Beavers said last year. "The third pitch hit me and knocked me out, so I don't remember much after that. I couldn't get in the sun for a while, and I never did play baseball again." Former minor leaguer Ron Shelton based the *Bull Durham* pitcher Nuke LaLoosh on Dalkowski. And yet, to see him as a figure of fun, an amusing loser, is to misunderstand something unique and strange.

Dalkowski kept on posting some of the strangest lines in baseball history. Pitching for the Stockton Ports of the Class C California League in 1960, he struck out 262 and walked 262 in 170 innings. Yet, he did improve, especially after pitching for Earl Weaver at Elmira in 1962. Weaver had previously had Dalkowski at Aberdeen in 1959, but wasn't ready to grapple with him then. This time he was. "I had grown more and more concerned about players with great physical abilities who could not learn to correct certain basic deficiencies no matter how much you instructed or drilled them," he related in his autobiography, *It's What You Learn After You Know It All That Counts*. He got permission from the Orioles to give all of his players the Stanford-Binet IQ test. "Dalkowski finished in the 1 percentile in his ability to understand facts. Steve, it was said to say, had the ability to do everything but learn." [sic]

IQ tests are problematic diagnostic tools, so take Weaver's estimate of Dalkowski's mental capabilities with a grain of salt. What's important is that even if he got to the right answer by way of the wrong reason, Weaver had learned something valuable. His insight was to stop asking Dalkowski to learn new pitches and just let him get by with the two that he had. Were Dalkowski a prospect today, that would have been a no-brainer: Can't develop a third pitch? The bullpen is right over there, sir. Player development wasn't like that then, but Weaver, temporarily Dalkowski's mentor, could let him work with what he had. According to Weaver, the pitcher responded: "In the final 57 innings he pitched that season Dalkowski gave up 1 earned run, struck out 110 batters, and walked only 11." It's not true—as per the *Elmira Star-Gazette*, as of late July, Dalkowski had walked 71 in 106 innings and finished with 114 in 160 innings, which means Dalkowski's control actually faded at the end of the season rather than improved—but that doesn't mean it didn't happen in some sense, just that it didn't happen that way. Again, it's the journey, not the destination, and his ERA was 3.04 so *something* had gone right.

Also along the way: The next spring, Orioles manager Billy Hitchcock was rooting for Dalkowski to make the team as a long-man—maybe Weaver had gotten through to him. There were things out of Weaver's control, like the universe's twisted sense of humor: that March, Dalkowski's elbow went "twang."

You sometimes read that it was the Orioles' insistence on Dalkowski learning the curve that did him in, but even if they hadn't learned their lesson, the injury was probably just a coincidence: Dalkowski had thrown an incredible number of pitches over the previous few years. Still, it testifies to the dangers of trying to get what you want and risking the loss of what you had. Dalkowski tried to come back, but the 110-mph stuff was gone. A pitcher with no control and no stuff is…a civilian. What followed were years of vagabond living, arrests for drunkenness. There were Alcoholics Anonymous meetings, assistance from baseball alumni associations, but none of it took. From the 1990s until the time of his passing he dwelt in an assisted living facility, suffering from alcohol-related dementia. He'd been a heavy drinker since his teenage years. As with all those pitches per game, there was a price to be paid. You make choices on the journey and some of them are irrevocable. It's like a fairy tale: "Bite of poison apple? Don't mind if I do."

In the aforementioned *Sporting News* profile, Chuck Stevens, the head of the Association of Professional Ballplayers of America, a ballplayer charity, said, "I've got nothing against drinking. I do it myself sometimes. But, I don't condone common drunkenness. We went through lots of heartache and many dollars, but Dalkowski didn't want to help himself and we weren't going to keep him drunk." The journey is *un*like a fairy tale: No one will come along and kiss it better, not if they're busy forming judgments.

In the end, we are left with a sort of philosophical chicken/egg conundrum: Is failing to meet your goals evidence of unfulfilled potential or the lack of it? Isn't what you did by definition what you were capable of doing? Or could you have broken through to something better with the right help, the right lucky break? These are unanswerable questions, and how we try to answer them may say more about us than about the people we're judging.

No pitcher ever has it easy. *All* pitchers must work hard. *All* pitchers must refine their craft. It's almost never just about *stuff*. Dalkowski dreaming is no insult to the great pitchers who made it; from Pete Alexander to Max Scherzer, they have all earned their way up. And yet, if it is true that we can only do as much as we can do, then the journey would be more of an adventure, the ultimate triumph or defeat more noble, if like Dalkowski we lacked 100 percent of the confidence, the command, the self-possession, the commitment, the resistance to making bad decisions that so many great players possess—to be gloriously human. Or, to put it more succinctly, it would be fun to be able to throw as hard as any person ever has. Even if just for a moment, and even if nothing more came of it than that, no one could say you hadn't lived life to the fullest.

—*Steven Goldman is an author of Baseball Prospectus.*

A Reward For A Functioning Society

by Cory Frontin and Craig Goldstein

On July 5, Nationals reliever Sean Doolittle said in the middle of a press conference regarding the restart of Major League Baseball and what would later be known as summer camp, "sports are like the reward of a functioning society." This sentence was amidst a much longer, thoughtful reply about the societal and health conditions under which MLB players were being brought back. It's a very similar sentiment to one Jane McManus used on April 7, when she discussed the White House's meeting with sports commissioners. She said "sports are the effect of a functioning society—not the precursor."

Both versions of the same sentiment spoke to a laudable ideal in the context of a country that was not addressing a rampaging virus, and opting instead to bring sports back for the feeling of normalcy rather than the reality of it. "Priorities," as McManus said.

On Wednesday, the NBA's Milwaukee Bucks conducted a wildcat/political strike, refusing to come out for Game 5 of their playoff series against the Orlando Magic. The Magic refused to accept the forfeit, and shortly thereafter other playoff series were threatened by player strikes. Eventually the league moved to postpone that day's games, folding to players leveraging their united power.

The backdrop against which these actions took place was the shooting by police of Jacob Blake. Blake was shot in the back seven times by police, as he attempted to get into his vehicle. He managed to survive the assault, but is paralyzed from the waist down.

⚾ ⚾ ⚾

The step taken to walk out, first by the Milwaukee Bucks, then subsequently by other NBA, WNBA, and MLB teams, was a step toward upholding the virtue of the sentiment described by McManus and Doolittle. But that sentiment does not align with the broad history of sports in this and other countries, a history that contradicts the core of the idealistic statement.

Sports have been a significant part of American society for most of its existence, expanding in importance and influence in recent years. The idea that society was functioning in a way that was worthy of the reward of sports for most of that time is laughable. Much of America is not functioning and has not functioned for Black people, full stop. The oppressed people at the center of this political act by players, specifically Black players, in concert throughout the NBA and in fits and starts throughout Major League Baseball, have not known a society that functions for them rather than *because* of them.

Politics has been part of the sports landscape since the inception of sport, but for just about as long people have bemoaned its presence. Sports are to be an escape, it is said. An escape from what, though? A functioning society?

No, the presence of sports has never signified a cultural or political system that is on the up and up. Rather, the presence of sports *reflect and reinforce the society that produces them.*

⚾   ⚾   ⚾

The Negro Leagues were born out of societal dysfunction. The need for entirely separate leagues, composed of Black and Latino players barred from the Major Leagues because of racism? That is not a functioning society, and yet there were sports.

Even the integration of players from the Negro Leagues resulted in a transfer of power and wealth from Black-owned businesses and communities and into white ones, mirroring the dysfunction that had bled into every aspect of American society at the time. Japheth Knopp noted in the Spring 2016 Baseball Research Journal:

> *The manner in which integration in baseball—and in American businesses generally—occurred was not the only model which was possible. It was likely not even the best approach available, but rather served the needs of those in already privileged positions who were able to control not only the manner in which desegregation occurred, but the public perception of it as well in order to exploit the situation for financial gain. Indeed, the very word integration may not be the most applicable in this context because what actually transpired was not so much the fair and equitable combination of two subcultures into one equal and more homogenous group, but rather the reluctant allowance—under certain preconditions—for African Americans to be assimilated into white society.*

To understand the value of a movement, though, is not to understand how it is co-opted by ownership, but to know the people it brings together and what they demand. When Jackie Robinson—the player who demarcated the inevitability of the end of the Negro leagues—attended the March on Washington for Jobs and Freedom in 1963, he did so with his family and marched alongside the people. He stood alongside hundreds of thousands to fight for their common civil and labor rights. "The moral arc of the universe is long," many freedom fighters have echoed, "but it bends towards justice." The bend, it is less frequently said, happens when a great mass of people place the moral arc of the universe on their knee and apply force, as Jackie, his family, and thousands of others did that day.

⚾ ⚾ ⚾

Of course, taking the moral arc of the universe down from the mantle and bending it is not without risk. Perhaps the outsized influence of athletes is itself a mark of a dysfunctional society, but, nonetheless, hundreds of athletes woke up on Wednesday morning with the power to bring in millions of dollars in revenues. That very power, as we would come to find out, was matched with the equal and opposite power to *not* bring those revenues. That power, in hands ranging from the Milwaukee Bucks, to Kenny Smith in the *Inside the NBA* Studio, from the unexpected ally, Josh Hader, and his largely white teammates to the notably Black Seattle Mariners, would be exercised for a single demand: the end to state violence against Black people. Not unlike the March itself, it sat at the intersection of the civil rights of Black Americans and bold labor action. The March on Washington stood in the face of a false notion of integration—against an integration of extraction but not one of equality—and proposed something different. Just the same, the acts of solidarity of August 26, 2020 will be remembered in stark defiance of MLB's BLM-branded, but ultimately empty displays on opening weekend.

Bold defiance like this can never be without risk. By choosing to exercise this power, the Milwaukee Bucks took a risk. They risked vitriol and backlash from those they disagreed with. They risked fines or seeing their contracts voided, as a walkout like this is prohibited by their CBA. They risked forfeiting a playoff game, one that, as the No. 1 seed in the playoffs, they'd worked all year to attain. They didn't know how Orlando would respond. It wasn't clear that other teams throughout the league would follow suit in solidarity. And it wasn't known the league would accept these actions and moderately co-opt them by "postponing" games that would have featured no players.

If the league reschedules the games, some of the athletes' risk—their shared sacrifice—will be diminished, in retrospect. But they did not know any of that when they took that risk. And it is often left to athletes to take these risks when others in society won't, especially those of their same socioeconomic status and levels of influence.

It is athletes, specifically BIPOC athletes, that take them, though, because they live with the risk of being something other than white in this country every day. They are no strangers to the realities of police brutality. It seems incongruous

Atlanta Braves 2021

then, to say that sports are a reward for a functioning society when we rely on athletes to lead us closer to being a functioning society. Luckily, our beloved athletes, WNBA players first and foremost among them, understand what sports truly are: a pipebender for the moral arc of the universe.

—Craig Goldstein is editor in chief of Baseball Prospectus. Cory Frontin is an author of Baseball Prospectus.

Index of Names

Acuña Jr., Ronald	16	Markakis, Nick	32
Adrianza, Ehire	18	Martin, Chris	54
Albies, Ozzie	20	Matzek, Tyler	56
Almonte, Abraham	86	Mayfield, Jack	92
Anderson, Ian	40, 105	Melancon, Mark	58
Arano, Vìctor	98	Milone, Tommy	60
Backstrom, Mahki	113	Minter, A.J.	62
Ball, Bryce	113	Morton, Charlie	64
Camargo, Johan	22	Muller, Kyle	102, 107
Contreras, William	87, 109	Newcomb, Sean	66
d'Arnaud, Travis	24	Ozuna, Marcell	34
Davidson, Tucker	98, 109	Pache, Cristian	93, 106
Dayton, Grant	42	Riley, Austin	36
De La Cruz, Jasseel	99, 112	Rojas Jr., Mel	94
Demeritte, Travis	88	Sandoval, Pablo	95
Duvall, Adam	26	Shewmake, Braden	96, 110
Edwards Jr., Carl	100	Shuster, Jared	103, 111
Erlin, Robbie	44	Smith, Will	68
Flowers, Tyler	89	Smyly, Drew	70
Freeman, Freddie	28	Sobotka, Chad	103
Fried, Max	46	Soroka, Mike	72
Greene, Shane	48	Strider, Spencer	114
Hamels, Cole	101	Swanson, Dansby	38
Harris, Michael	111	Tomlin, Josh	74
Hechavarría, Adeiny	90	Toussaint, Touki	76
Inciarte, Ender	30	Waters, Drew	97, 107
Jackson, Alex	90, 113	Webb, Jacob	78
Jackson, Luke	50	Weigel, Patrick	104, 112
Jones, Nate	52	Wilson, Bryse	80
Kipnis, Jason	91	Wright, Kyle	82
Langeliers, Shea	92, 108	Ynoa, Huascar	84

For the Joy of Keeping Score

THIRTY81 Project is an ongoing graphic design project focused on the ballparks of baseball. Since being established in 2013, scorecards have been a fundemantal part of the effort. Each two-page card is uniquely ballpark-centric — there are 30 variants — and designed with both beginning and veteran scorekeepers in mind. Evolving over the years with suggestions from fans, broadcasters, and official scorers, the sheets are freely available to everyone as printable letter-size PDFs at the project webshop at www.THIRTY81Project.com

Download, Print, Score, Repeat ...

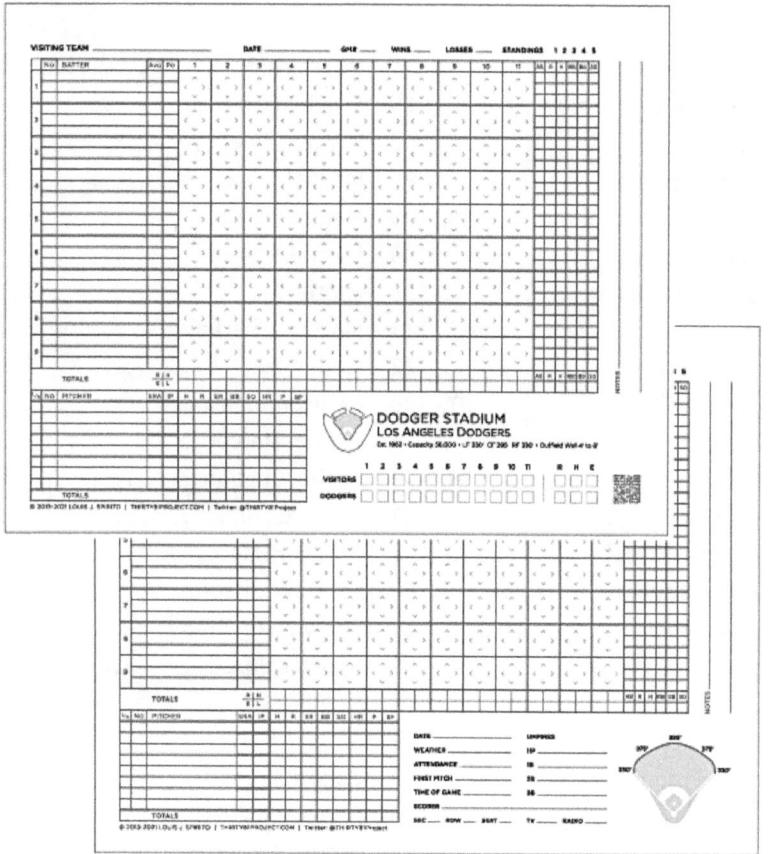

Scorecard design ©2013-2021 Louis J. Spirito | THIRTY81Project